Complete
MONTH OF MEALS
COLLECTION

AMERICAN DIABETES ASSOCIATION

**American
Diabetes
Association**®

Director, Book Publishing, Abe Ogden; *Managing Editor and Project Manager,* Rebekah Renshaw; *Acquisitions Editor,* Victor Van Beuren; *Production Manager,* Melissa Sprott; *Composition and Cover Design,* pixiedesign llc; *Photographer,* Tara Donne Photography; *Recipe Developer,* Barbara Seelig-Brown; *Printer,* Imago.

Printed in China
1 3 5 7 9 10 8 6 4 2

The suggestions and information contained in this publication are generally consistent with the *Standards of Medical Care in Diabetes* and other policies of the American Diabetes Association, but they do not represent the policy or position of the Association or any of its boards or committees. Reasonable steps have been taken to ensure the accuracy of the information presented. However, the American Diabetes Association cannot ensure the safety or efficacy of any product or service described in this publication. Individuals are advised to consult a physician or other appropriate health care professional before undertaking any diet or exercise program or taking any medication referred to in this publication. Professionals must use and apply their own professional judgment, experience, and training and should not rely solely on the information contained in this publication before prescribing any diet, exercise, or medication. The American Diabetes Association—its officers, directors, employees, volunteers, and members—assumes no responsibility or liability for personal or other injury, loss, or damage that may result from the suggestions or information in this publication.

♾ The paper in this publication meets the requirements of the ANSI Standard Z39.48-1992 (permanence of paper).

ADA titles may be purchased for business or promotional use or for special sales. To purchase more than 50 copies of this book at a discount, or for custom editions of this book with your logo, contact the American Diabetes Association at the address below or at booksales@diabetes.org.

American Diabetes Association
2451 Crystal Drive, Suite 900
Arlington, VA 22202

DOI: 10.2337/9781580406628

Library of Congress Cataloging-in-Publication Data
  Names: American Diabetes Association.
  Title: The complete month of meals collection : hundreds of diabetes-friendly
    recipes and nearly limitless meal combinations / American Diabetes
    Association.
  Description: Arlington [Virginia] : American Diabetes Association, [2017]
  Identifiers: LCCN 2016058163 | ISBN 9781580406628
  Subjects: LCSH: Diabetes--Diet therapy--Recipes. | LCGFT: Cookbooks.
  Classification: LCC RC662 .C627 2017 | DDC 641.5/6314--dc23
  LC record available at https://lccn.loc.gov/2016058163

Table of Contents

Scones, pg. 103

Stuffed Peppers, pg. 117

What Can I Eat?

Are you constantly asking yourself, "What can I eat?" If so, it's time to stop worrying! Living with diabetes doesn't mean you have to feel deprived. Knowing what to eat when you have diabetes can be confusing. Everywhere you turn, there is news about what is or isn't good for you. But a few basic tips have weathered the fad diets, and have withstood the test of time.

Once you get the hang of eating a healthy diet, you can relax and dig in to a wide variety of delicious meals and snacks.

DIABETES SUPERFOODS

Ever see the top 10 lists for foods everyone should eat to superpower their diet? Ever wonder which will mesh with your diabetes meal plan? Wonder no more. Your list of the top 10 diabetes superfoods has arrived.

As with all foods, you need to work the diabetes superfoods into your individualized meal plan in the right proportions.

All of the foods in our list have a lower impact on your blood glucose and provide key nutrients that are lacking in the typical western diet such as:

- calcium
- potassium
- fiber
- magnesium
- vitamins A (as carotenoids), C, and E.

There isn't research that clearly points to any benefits of using supplements, so always think first about getting your nutrients from foods. Below is our list of superfoods to include in your diet.

BEANS

Whether you prefer kidney, pinto, navy, or black beans, you can't find better nutrition than that provided by beans. They are very high in fiber, giving you about 1/3 of your daily requirement in just a 1/2 cup, and are also good sources of protein, magnesium, and potassium.

While beans do have an impact on blood glucose, they are considered "legumes" technically and fit best in the starchy vegetable category, but 1/2 cup provides as much protein as an ounce of meat without the saturated fat. To save time you can use canned beans, but be sure to drain and rinse them to get rid of as much sodium as possible.

DARK GREEN LEAFY VEGETABLES

Spinach, collards, kale, arugula—these powerhouse foods are so low in calories and carbohydrate.

CITRUS FRUIT

Oranges, lemons, and limes. Pick your favorites and get part of your daily dose of soluble fiber and vitamin C.

SWEET POTATOES

A starchy vegetable packed full of vitamin A and fiber.

BERRIES

Which are your favorites: blueberries, strawberries, or another variety? Regardless, they are all packed with antioxidants, vitamins, and fiber. Berries are also lower in carbohydrate than many other fruits.

TOMATOES

An old standby where everyone can find a favorite. The good news is that no matter how you like your tomatoes, pureed, raw, or in a sauce, you're eating vital nutrients like vitamin C, iron, vitamin E.

FISH HIGH IN OMEGA-3 FATTY ACIDS

Salmon is a favorite in this category, but there are others too like sardines, herring, mackerel, and albacore tuna. Stay away from the breaded and deep fat fried variety—they don't count in your goal of 6–9 ounces of fish per week.

WHOLE GRAINS

It's the germ and bran of the whole grain you're after. It contains all the nutrients a grain product has to offer. When you purchase processed grains, like bread made from enriched wheat flour, the germ and bran have been removed. A few more of the nutrients these foods offer are magnesium, chromium, omega-3 fatty acids, and folate.

Pearled barley and oatmeal are a source of fiber and potassium.

NUTS

An ounce of nuts can go a long way in providing key healthy fats along with hunger management. Other benefits are a dose of magnesium and fiber.

Some nuts and seeds, such as walnuts and flax seeds, also contain omega-3 fatty acids.

FAT-FREE MILK AND YOGURT

Everyone knows dairy can help build strong bones and teeth. In addition to calcium, many fortified dairy products are a good source of vitamin D. More research is emerging on the connection between vitamin D and good health.

Some of the above list can be tough on the budget, depending on the season and where you live. Look for lower-cost options such as fruit and vegetables in season or frozen or canned fish.

Foods that every budget can live with year round are beans and rolled oats or barley that you cook from scratch.

Making Healthy Food Choices

NON-STARCHY VEGETABLES

Eat more! You don't often hear that when you have diabetes, but non-starchy vegetables are one food group where you can satisfy your appetite.

Vegetables are full of vitamins, minerals, fiber, and phytochemicals—and with so few calories and carbohydrate, everyone can enjoy more!

There are two main types of vegetables—starchy and non-starchy. For this section, we are going to focus only on the non-starchy vegetables.

WHAT ARE THE BEST CHOICES?

The best choices are fresh, frozen, and canned vegetables without added sodium, fat, or sugar.

- If using canned or frozen vegetables, look for ones that say low sodium or no salt added on the label.
- As a general rule, frozen or canned vegetables in sauces are higher in both fat and sodium.
- If using canned vegetables with sodium, drain the vegetables and rinse with water. Then cook the rinsed vegetables in fresh water. This will cut back on how much sodium is left on the vegetables.

For good health, try to eat at least 3–5 servings of vegetables a day. This is a minimum and more is better! A serving of vegetables is:

- 1/2 cup of cooked vegetables
- 1 cup of raw vegetables

COMMON NON-STARCHY VEGETABLES

The following is a list of common non-starchy vegetables:

- Amaranth or Chinese spinach
- Artichoke
- Artichoke hearts
- Asparagus
- Baby corn
- Bamboo shoots
- Beans (green, wax, Italian)
- Bean sprouts
- Beets
- Brussels sprouts
- Broccoli
- Cabbage (green, bok choy, Chinese)
- Carrots
- Cauliflower
- Celery
- Chayote
- Coleslaw (packaged, no dressing)
- Cucumber
- Daikon
- Eggplant
- Greens (collard, kale, mustard, turnip)
- Hearts of palm

- Jicama
- Kohlrabi
- Leeks
- Mushrooms
- Okra
- Onions
- Pea pods
- Peppers
- Radishes
- Rutabaga
- Salad greens (chicory, endive, escarole, lettuce, romaine, spinach, arugula, radicchio, watercress)
- Sprouts
- Squash (cushaw, summer, crookneck, spaghetti, zucchini)
- Sugar snap peas
- Swiss chard
- Tomato
- Turnips
- Water chestnuts
- Yard-long beans

FRUITS

Wondering if you can eat fruit? Yes! Fruits are loaded with vitamins, minerals, and fiber just like vegetables.

Fruit contains carbohydrate so they do affect your blood glucose. Having a piece of fresh fruit or fruit salad for dessert is a great way to satisfy your sweet tooth and get the extra nutrition you're looking for.

WHAT ARE THE BEST CHOICES?

The best choices of fruit are any that are fresh, frozen, or canned without added sugars.

- Choose canned fruits in juice or light syrup

- Dried fruit can be a nutritious choice, but the portion sizes are small, so they may not be as filling as other choices.

COMMON FRUITS

The following is a list of common fruits:

- Apples
- Applesauce
- Apricots
- Avocado
- Banana
- Blackberries
- Blueberries
- Cantaloupe
- Cherries
- Dried fruit such as:
  - Cherries
  - Cranberries
  - Dates
  - Figs
  - Prunes
  - Raisins
- Grapefruit
- Grapes
- Honeydew melon
- Kiwi
- Mango
- Nectarine
- Orange
- Papaya
- Peaches
- Pears
- Pineapple
- Plums
- Raspberries
- Strawberries
- Tangerines
- Watermelon

GRAINS AND STARCHY VEGETABLES

One thing is for sure. If you are going to eat grain foods, pick the ones that are the most nutritious. Choose whole grains. Whole grains are rich in vitamins, minerals, phytochemicals, and fiber.

Reading labels is essential for this food group to make sure you are making the best choices.

Every time you choose to eat a starchy food, make it count! Leave the processed white flour–based products, especially the ones with added sugar, on the shelves or use them only for special occasion treats.

WHAT IS A WHOLE GRAIN?

A whole grain is the entire grain—which includes the bran, germ, and endosperm (starchy part).

The most popular grain in the U.S. is wheat, so that will be our example. To make 100% whole-wheat flour, the entire wheat grain is ground up. "Refined" flours like white and enriched wheat flour include only part of the grain—the starchy part, and are not whole grain. They are missing many of the nutrients found in whole-wheat flour.

Examples of whole-grain wheat products include 100% whole-wheat bread, pasta, tortillas, and crackers. But don't stop there! There are many whole grains to choose from.

WHAT ARE THE BEST CHOICES?

Finding whole-grain foods can be a challenge. Some foods only contain a small amount of whole grain but will say it contains whole grain on the front of the package. For all cereals and grains, read the ingredient list and look for the following sources of whole grains as the first ingredient:

- Bulgur (cracked wheat)
- Whole-wheat flour
- Whole oats/oatmeal
- Whole-grain corn/corn meal
- Popcorn
- Brown rice
- Whole rye
- Whole-grain barley
- Whole farro
- Wild rice
- Buckwheat
- Buckwheat flour
- Triticale
- Millet
- Quinoa
- Sorghum

Most rolls, breads, cereals, and crackers labeled as "made with" or "containing" whole grain do not have whole grain as the first ingredient. Read labels carefully to find the most nutritious grain products.

For cereals, pick those with at least 3 grams of fiber per serving and less than 6 grams of sugar.

STARCHY VEGETABLES

Starchy vegetables are great sources of vitamins, minerals, and fiber. The best choices do not have added fats, sugar, or sodium.

Try a variety such as:
- Parsnip
- Plantain
- Potato
- Pumpkin
- Acorn squash
- Butternut squash
- Green Peas
- Corn

DRIED BEANS, LEGUMES, PEAS, AND LENTILS

Try to include dried beans in several meals per week. They are a great source of protein and are loaded with fiber, vitamins, and minerals.

- Dried beans such as black, lima, and pinto
- Lentils
- Dried peas such as black-eyed and split
- Fat-free refried beans

PROTEIN FOODS

Foods high in protein such as fish, chicken, meats, soy products, and cheese, are all called "protein foods." You may also hear them referred to as "meats or meat substitutes."

The biggest difference among foods in this group is how much fat they contain, and for the vegetarian proteins, whether they have carbohydrate.

BEST PROTEIN CHOICES

The best choices are:

- Plant-based proteins
- Fish and seafood (not fried)
- Chicken and other poultry
- Eggs

PLANT-BASED PROTEINS

Plant-based protein foods provide quality protein, healthy fats, and fiber. They vary in how much fat and carbohydrate they contain, so make sure to read labels.

- Beans such as black, kidney, and pinto
- Bean products like baked beans and refried beans
- Hummus and falafel
- Lentils such as brown, green, or yellow
- Peas such as black-eyed or split peas

- Edamame
- Soy nuts
- Nuts and spreads like almond butter, cashew butter, or peanut butter
- Tempeh, tofu
- Products like meatless "chicken" nuggets, "beef" crumbles, "burgers," "bacon," "sausage," and "hot dogs," but be sure to read the Nutrition Facts Label; just because a food is a meat alternative does not guarantee it is low in saturated fat.

FISH AND SEAFOOD

Try to include fish at least 2 times per week.

- Fish high in omega-3 fatty acids like albacore tuna, herring, mackerel, rainbow trout, sardines, and salmon
- Other fish including catfish, cod, flounder, haddock, halibut, orange roughy, and tilapia
- Shellfish including clams, crab, imitation shellfish, lobster, scallops, shrimp, oysters

POULTRY

Choose poultry without the skin for less saturated fat and cholesterol.

- Chicken, turkey, cornish hen

CHEESE AND EGGS

- Use reduced-fat cheese or use less of a stronger cheese
- Cottage cheese
- Egg whites and egg substitutes

GAME

- Buffalo/bison, rabbit, venison, elk

BEEF, PORK, VEAL, LAMB

In general, these red meats tend to be higher in saturated fat. If you decide to have these, choose the leanest options, which are:

- Select or Choice grades of beef trimmed of fat, including: chuck, rib, rump roast, round, sirloin, cubed, flank, porterhouse, T-bone steak, tenderloin
- Beef jerky
- Lamb: chop, leg, or roast
- Organ meats: heart, kidney, liver
- Veal: loin chop or roast
- Pork: Canadian bacon, center loin chop, ham, tenderloin

DAIRY

Including sources of dairy in your diet is an easy way to get calcium and high-quality protein.

WHAT ARE THE BEST CHOICES?

The best choices of dairy products are:

- Fat-free or low-fat (1% milk)
- Plain nonfat yogurt (regular or Greek)
- Nonfat light yogurt (regular or Greek)
- Unflavored fortified soy milk

If you are lactose intolerant or don't like milk, you may want to try fortified soy milk, rice milk, or almond milk as a source of calcium and vitamin D.

GENERAL TIPS

- Each 1-cup serving of milk or 6-ounce serving of yogurt has about 12 grams of carbohydrate and 8 grams of protein.
- If you are trying to switch to lower-fat dairy products, take the time to get used to the taste and texture difference. For example, first change from whole milk to 2%. Then to 1% or nonfat milk.
- Switching from whole to 1% milk will save you 70 calories and 4 grams of saturated fat in every 8-ounce serving!

FATS

No doubt about it, carbohydrate gets all of the attention in diabetes management. However, fat also plays a big part in weight gain and diabetes risk. More important than total fat is the type of fat you eat. There are "healthy fats" and "unhealthy fats."

To lower your risk of heart disease, try to eat less saturated and trans fat—the unhealthy fats. At the same time, you can protect your heart by eating more mono- and polyunsaturated fats, including omega-3s—the healthy fats.

It is true that all fat is high in calories so it is important to watch portion sizes as well, but you can keep your calories the same by cutting back on the sources of saturated and trans fats, while substituting the healthy fats in their place. For example, instead of 1 cheese stick for an afternoon snack, have 12 almonds. The calories are about the same, but you will be getting more heart-healthy fats in place of saturated fats.

UNHEALTHY FATS

Saturated Fat

Why should you eat less saturated fat? Because saturated fat raises blood cholesterol levels. High blood cholesterol is a risk factor for heart disease. People with diabetes are at high risk for heart disease and limiting your saturated fat can help lower your risk of having a heart attack or stroke.

Foods containing saturated fat include:

- Lard
- Fatback and salt pork
- High-fat meats like regular ground beef, bologna, hot dogs, sausage, bacon, and spareribs

- Full-fat dairy products such as cheese, cream, ice cream, whole milk, 2% milk, and sour cream.
- Butter
- Cream sauces
- Gravy made with meat drippings
- Chocolate
- Palm oil and palm kernel oil
- Coconut and coconut oil
- Poultry (chicken and turkey) skin

The goal for people with and without diabetes is to eat less than 10% of calories from saturated fat. As a point of reference, this amounts to about 20 grams of saturated fat per day for an average adult. That is not much when you consider just one ounce of cheese can have 8 grams of saturated fat.

Many adults, especially women or sedentary men, may need less. To find out a specific goal for you, talk with your dietitian or health-care provider.

Saturated fat grams are listed on the Nutrition Facts food label under total fat. As a general rule, compare foods with less saturated fat. Foods with 1 gram or less saturated fat per serving are considered low in saturated fat.

HEALTHY FATS

Monounsaturated Fat

Monounsaturated fats are called "good" or "healthy" fats because they can lower your bad (LDL) cholesterol. Sources of monounsaturated fat include:

- Avocado
- Canola oil
- Nuts like almonds, cashews, pecans, and peanuts
- Olive oil and olives
- Peanut butter and peanut oil
- Sesame seeds

The American Diabetes Association recommends eating more monounsaturated fats than saturated or trans fats in your diet.

To include more monounsaturated fats, try to substitute olive or canola oil instead of butter, margarine, or shortening when cooking. Sprinkling a few nuts or sunflower seeds on a salad, yogurt, or cereal is an easy way to eat more monounsaturated fats.

But be careful! Nuts and oils are high in calories, like all fats. If you are trying to lose or maintain your weight, you want to eat small portions of these foods. For example, 6 almonds or 4 pecan halves have the same calories as 1 teaspoon of oil or butter.

Work with your dietitian to include healthy fats into your meal plan without increasing your total calories.

Monounsaturated fats are not required on the label, but many foods that are a good source do list them.

Polyunsaturated Fat

Polyunsaturated fats are also "healthy" fats. The ADA recommends that you include these in your diet as well as monounsaturated fats. Like the other healthy fats, you want to replace the sources of saturated fat in your diet with polyunsaturated fats.

Sources of polyunsaturated fats are:

- Corn oil
- Cottonseed oil
- Safflower oil
- Soybean oil
- Sunflower oil
- Walnuts

- Pumpkin or sunflower seeds
- Soft (tub) margarine
- Mayonnaise
- Salad dressings

Omega-3 Fatty Acids

Omega-3 fatty acids help prevent clogging of the arteries. Some types of fish are high in omega-3 fatty acids. The Association recommends eating non-fried fish 2 or 3 times a week.

Sources include:
- Albacore tuna
- Herring
- Mackerel
- Rainbow trout
- Sardines
- Salmon

Some plant foods are also sources of omega-3 fatty acids. Sources include:
- Tofu and other soybean products
- Walnuts
- Flaxseed and flaxseed oil
- Canola oil

NOTE: The Food & Drug Administration and the Environmental Protection Agency have issued a joint consumer advisory about eating fish. This advice is geared toward helping women who are pregnant or may become pregnant—as well as breastfeeding mothers and parents of young children—make informed choices when it comes to fish that is healthy and safe to eat.

For women of childbearing age (about 16–49 years old), especially pregnant and breastfeeding women, and for parents and caregivers of young children:

- Eat 2 to 3 servings of fish a week from the "Best Choices" list OR 1 serving from the "Good Choices" list.
- Eat a variety of fish.
- Serve 1 to 2 servings of fish a week to children, starting at age 2.
- If you eat fish caught by family or friends, check for fish advisories. If there is no advisory, eat only 1 serving and no other fish that week.

You can use the chart below to help you choose which fish to eat, and how often to eat them, based on their mercury levels.

BEST CHOICES
EAT 2 TO 3 SERVINGS A WEEK

Anchovy	Herring	Scallop
Atlantic croaker	Lobster, American and spiny	Shad
Atlantic mackerel	Mullet	Shrimp
Black sea bass	Oyster	Skate
Butterfish	Pacific chub mackerel	Smelt
Catfish		Sole
Clam	Perch, freshwater and ocean	Squid
Cod		Tilapia
Crab	Pickerel	Trout, freshwater
Crawfish	Plaice	Tuna, canned light (includes skipjack)
Flounder	Pollock	
Haddock	Salmon	Whitefish
Hake	Sardine	Whiting

OR

GOOD CHOICES
EAT 1 SERVING WEEK

Bluefish	Monkfish	Tilefish (Atlantic Ocean)
Buffalofish	Rockfish	Tuna, albacore/white tuna, canned and fresh/frozen
Carp	Sablefish	
Chilean sea bass/ Patagonian toothfish	Sheepshead	
	Snapper	Tuna, yellowfin
Grouper	Spanish mackerel	Weakfish/seatrout
Halibut	Striped bass (ocean)	White croaker/Pacific croaker
Mahi mahi/dolphinfish		

CHOICES TO AVOID
HIGHEST MERCURY LEVELS

King mackerel	Shark	Tilefish (Gulf of Mexico)
Marlin	Swordfish	
Orange roughy		Tuna, bigeye

Adapted from "Advice About Eating Fish" from www.fda.gov/fishadvice

The "Best Choices" have the lowest levels of mercury.

A good visual reference for fish serving sizes is the palm of your hand:

- An adult serving size is 4 ounces.
- For children ages 4 to 7, a serving size is 2 ounces.

4 ounces
ADULT SERVING **2 ounces**
CHILD (4–7) SERVING

ALCOHOL

Wondering if alcohol is off limits with diabetes? Most people with diabetes can have a moderate amount of alcohol. Research has shown that there can be some health benefits such as reducing risk for heart disease. But, moderation is important. If you have any questions about whether alcohol is safe for you, check with your doctor. People with diabetes should follow the same guidelines as those without diabetes if they choose to drink:

- Women should have no more than 1 drink per day.
- Men should have no more than 2 drinks per day.

One drink is equal to a 12-oz beer, 5-oz glass of wine, or 1.5-oz distilled spirits (vodka, whiskey, gin, etc.).

SOME TIPS TO SIP BY

- If you have diabetes, practice caution when drinking. Do not drink on an empty stomach or when your blood glucose is low. If you choose to drink, follow the guidelines above and have it with food. This is especially important for those on insulin and diabetes pills that lower blood glucose.
- Do not omit food from your regular meal plan to replace it with alcohol. (If you use carbohydrate counting to plan meals, do not count alcohol in your plan as a carbohydrate choice.)
- Wear an I.D. that notes you have diabetes.
- Sip your drink slowly to savor it and make it last.
- Have a zero-calorie beverage by your side to keep yourself hydrated, like water, diet soda, or iced tea.
- Try a light beer or wine spritzer made with wine, ice cubes, and club soda. Watch out for heavy craft beers, which can have twice the alcohol and calories as a light beer.
- For mixed drinks, choose calorie-free drink mixers like diet soda, club soda, diet tonic water, or water.
- Do not drive or plan to drive after you drink alcohol.

Alcohol can cause hypoglycemia shortly after drinking and for up to 24 hours after drinking. If you are going to drink alcohol, check your blood glucose before you drink, while you drink, and for up to 24 hours. You should also check your blood glucose before you go to bed to make sure it is at a safe level—between 100 and 140 mg/dL. If your blood glucose is low, eat something to raise it.

The symptoms of too much alcohol and hypoglycemia can be similar—sleepiness, dizziness, and disorientation. You do not want anyone to confuse hypoglycemia for drunkenness, because they might not give you the proper assistance and treatment. The best way to get the help you need if you are hypoglycemic is to always wear an I.D. that says "I have diabetes."

Alcohol may lessen your resolve to stay on track with healthy eating. If you plan to have a glass of wine at dinner or if you are going out for the night, plan ahead so you'll be able to stick to your usual meal plan and won't be tempted to overindulge.

WHAT CAN I DRINK?

Food often takes center stage when it comes to diabetes. But don't forget that the beverages you drink can also have an effect on your weight and blood glucose!

We recommend choosing zero-calorie or very low-calorie drinks. This includes:

- Water
- Unsweetened teas
- Coffee
- Diet soda
- Other low-calorie drinks and drink mixes

You can also try flavoring your water with a squeeze of lemon or lime juice for a light, refreshing drink with some flavor. All of these drinks provide minimal calories and carbohydrate.

WHAT TO AVOID

Avoid sugary drinks like regular soda, fruit punch, fruit drinks, energy drinks, sweet tea, and other sugary drinks. These will raise blood glucose and can provide several hundred calories in just one serving! See for yourself:

- One 12-ounce can of regular soda has about 150 calories and 40 grams of carbohydrate. This is the same amount of carbohydrate in 10 teaspoons of sugar!
- One cup of fruit punch and other sugary fruit drinks have about 100 calories (or more) and 30 grams of carbohydrate.

TIRED OF WATER?

As you can see, you have many other options!

Mix it up by choosing unsweetened teas. Hot or cold—black, green, and herbal teas provide lots of variety. You could also try sparkling water or making your own infused water at home. To make infused water, simply put water in the fridge with cucumbers, strawberries, or fresh mint for a refreshing low-calorie drink.

Most diet drinks (like diet soda or diet tea) have zero grams of carbohydrate per serving, so they will not raise blood glucose on their own. These diet drinks are sweetened with nonnutritive sweeteners instead of added sugars. Removing the added sugars and replacing them with low-calorie sweeteners removes most of the calories and carbohydrates.

Other low-calorie drinks and drink mixes are available in several flavors. They may be a good alternative to regular lemonade, iced tea, fruit punch, etc. These drinks also use low- or no-calorie sweeteners in place of sugar. They are very low in calories (about 5–10 calories per 8-ounce portion) and have less than 5 grams of carbohydrate per serving.

How To Use This Cookbook

Most cookbooks give you lots of recipes and only a few suggestions for combining them into a day's meals. When you find a recipe you like, you still must choose other foods to round out the meal. Many people with diabetes have the added challenge of counting the carbohydrate in the meal so they'll know what effect it will have on their blood glucose level. A simple but unexciting solution is to eat the same things day after day.

The American Diabetes Association's Complete Month of Meals Collection will help you choose healthy foods so you can easily create daily menus. You will find many menus that can be prepared quickly, menus built around favorite family dishes, meatless menus, and menus emphasizing low-fat and high-fiber foods. For people who cook for just one or two, most of these recipes can be prepared and then divided into individual servings and frozen for quick, no-fuss future meals.

There are complete menus for breakfast, lunch, and dinner, along with additional chapters with options for desserts, drinks, sides and salads, and more. You can mix and match one day's menu selections—breakfast, lunch, and dinner—to match your calorie goal for that day.

If you're counting carbohydrates (carb counting), counting fat grams, or simply counting calories, these numbers are clearly indicated for each complete meal. Knowing these totals for each meal and snack and keeping these totals consistent can have a great effect on your health!

These menus will help you

- *Eat a variety of foods.* Eating a wide variety of different foods helps you get all the essential vitamins, minerals, and nutrients your body needs. Variety also helps keep you interested, so your diet doesn't become boring. With these menus, you can create thousands of combinations of breakfasts, lunches, and dinners.

- *Maintain a healthy weight.* The Month of Meals system allows you to add and subtract snacks to get just the right number of calories for you to achieve and maintain a healthy body weight.

- *Choose a meal plan low in total and saturated fat.* The meals in this book average less than 30% total fat. These menus also emphasize low-fat foods.

- *Eat plenty of vegetables, fruits, and whole-grain products.* These foods not only add variety to your diet, but they also can be an important source of fiber. Unrefined foods are close in form to what Mother Nature gives us, and the closer to the source, the better.

- *Sugar is a hot topic these days.* It's okay to include some sugar as part of a balanced meal, but the calories add up quickly and sugar contributes to the total carbohydrate in your diet. That's why most of these recipes are low in sugar. Instead of sugar, you can also use sugar substitutes that have essentially no calories.

- *Watch sodium levels in processed foods.* Although packaged and fast foods are convenient, they can be high in added salt. If you need to watch your sodium intake, check package labels carefully. In general, though, sodium recommendations for people with diabetes (without hypertension) are the same as those for the general population, below 2300 mg/day. (If you have diabetes and hypertension, check with your doctor or dietitian to find out how much sodium you should be consuming each day.)

USING LABELING LINGO

As you use this book, you will see many familiar brand name items from the grocery store shelves. This is because we know that you want to use convenience foods on your busy days and that it is unrealistic to expect anyone to cook from scratch every day!

A trip to the grocery store can give you information overload: there are thousands of food products to choose from in the 30 minutes or so you have for shopping. Certainly, it is an information-processing nightmare to read all the labels and sort out the healthiest foods from the rest. So, average shoppers usually just resort to buying familiar products they have selected in the past, giving up on attempting to interpret these new products. Adding to the confusion are the nonnutritive sweeteners and low-fat products and their accompanying label claims…what's a health-conscious person to do?

At the start of your next trip, remember to shop the perimeter of the store first: most grocery stores are organized such that the basic four food groups line the four enclosing walls—produce, dairy, meat, and breads. Fill your cart with these nutritious essentials first, then proceed down only the aisles necessary to complete your grocery list. Pick one or two items to focus your label reading on each shopping trip. This habit will assure that you find a variety of healthy foods to meet your nutrient needs successfully each day.

Be sure to pay attention to the portion sizes listed on the food label by the manufacturer. All of the nutrition information on a label relates back to that portion. This is important if you are to be able to fit that food into your meal plan. Sometimes, it is not worth it if the portion is just too small.

USING PLANNED LEFTOVERS

Do you usually cook for one or two people, but all of your favorite recipes make six or eight servings? What should you do with the rest of the servings? The answer is to make planned-overs. Making planned-overs, or planning ahead with leftovers, is a great way to save steps in preparing meals and will also help you and your family follow a healthy eating plan.

Any recipes in this book that makes more servings than you need can become a planned-over. If you're following the recipe for Old-Fashioned Pot Roast (page D20), which makes eight servings, but only need two servings, portion the remainder of the cooked meat (after you remove the fat) into six servings. Undercook about three-quarters of the vegetables; they will finish cooking as you reheat, and nothing says "leftovers" more than mushy vegetables. Package the meals, adding 2 ounces of gravy on top of each, for the freezer. A dinner portion consists of about 3 ounces of cooked meat (the size of a deck of cards), 2/3 to 1 cup of a starchy or carbohydrate-based food item, 1 cup of vegetables, and a total of 2 servings of fats. If your planned-over isn't totally complete, plan to add fresh foods when you serve it, such as fresh fruit for dessert and a green salad with 1 tablespoon of dressing.

When deciding how to store the servings, think about how you'll reheat them. The most convenient way is to store planned-overs in the same container you will use to reheat. Aluminum foil is great for a conventional oven. Newer plastic containers are freezer and microwave safe and make for easy reheating. Another method is to store each portion in a freezer storage bag and reheat it in another dish once it's thawed. You can thaw the meals quickly in the microwave (but be sure to use the defrost cycle or you will overcook the outside while the inside of the food remains frozen) or set them in the refrigerator the night before or first thing in the morning to thaw.

It's tempting to let your future planned-overs sit cooling on the stove while you eat.

However, bacteria grow quickly at warm and room temperatures. It's best to pack and store your planned-overs before you start to eat your meal. (This also cuts down on the temptation to have a little more after you eat.) Foods cool more quickly when refrigerated in small shallow containers versus large containers, reducing the chance of spoiled food.

Once you've put planned-overs in the freezer or refrigerator, don't forget them! Keeping foods too long in the freezer leads to taste loss, and if they sit too long in the refrigerator, the food can go bad. The pot roast planned-over above will last about 2–3 months in the freezer without losing its taste but only about 3–4 days in the refrigerator without spoiling.

Because every microwave is a little bit different, experiment when thawing and reheating.

Breads and muffins should be loosely wrapped in a napkin or microwave-safe paper towel. Keep the wrapping on the bread for a bit after you've taken it out of the oven—this keeps the steam inside the bread instead of letting it escape. One muffin will heat in about 20 seconds; if you have two, don't double the time—30 seconds will do nicely. Overheating breads in the microwave makes them tough. You may also want to try heating breads on a low or defrost setting for a longer time to avoid chewiness. When you have several frozen muffins or rolls, arrange them in a circle and rotate or turn them over halfway through the cooking time.

After this small amount of planning ahead, you start to reap the benefits:

- Meals, in a healthy portion size, are ready when you are.
- Your meal can be eaten without the temptation of having seconds.
- Preparing and portioning ahead can help strengthen your resolve to follow your meal plan.
- Some foods, especially soups and those in a sauce or gravy, simply taste better in a day or two, when you've given the seasonings time to blend.
- You can enjoy most recipes even though you only need one or two servings at a time.

FOLLOWING YOUR CALORIE REQUIREMENTS

This book allows you to choose the calorie level that best meets your needs. First, you need to know how many calories you require daily. The best way to do this is to meet with a registered dietitian or certified diabetes educator, who can design a meal plan with the right number of calories for your nutritional needs.

BASIC MEAL PLAN: 1,500 CALORIES A DAY

Each breakfast, lunch, and dinner meal has about the same number of calories as the other breakfasts, lunches, or dinners, respectively, so you can mix and match them to suit your own tastes. All the portions on the menus are for one person, so you can have everything listed. If you need more or fewer calories than this, no problem. Adjusting meals to meet your requirements is easy.

OTHER CALORIE LEVELS: 1,200, 1,800, AND 2,100 CALORIES A DAY

Your dietitian or diabetes educator may recommend that you follow a diet with a different calorie limit per day. If that applies to you, it's still easy to use these menus. Just use the Menu Tracker on page 18 to adjust the meal plan to suit your needs.

For example, if you are following a meal plan that allows you 1,800 calories a day, here is how you would adjust the Basic Meal Plan using the chart.

1. Choose any menus that you want to fill out the day's meals.
2. If you have leftover unused calories after you pick your breakfast, lunch, and dinner, pick side, salad, dessert, or drink to round out your calories for the day.

If your health-care team recommends that you follow a 1,200-calorie diet, then for the most part, you can just prepare the menus as they appear in the book. Your meal plan will not have any snacks or sides. You may have to adjust menus to reduce the calorie content, however, so pay close attention to the next section: Adjusting Your Menus.

If you have been placed on a 2,000- or 2,100-calorie diet, you'll have to increase the caloric content of your meals. Again, you'll need to add other sides or snacks throughout the day to fill out your plan. For instructions on how to do that, go to the next section: Adjusting Your Menus.

ADJUSTING YOUR MENUS

There will be instances where the recipes and menus you pick for a certain day will provide either too few or too many calories or carbohydrates. As you have seen from the chart showing you how to follow different diets of different caloric levels, you may need to add a serving of food to your menus.

The menus in this book have been developed using a meal-planning system that divides foods into separate groups: Starch, Fruit, Milk, Vegetables, Meat and Meat Substitutes, and Fat. Foods are placed into one group or another based on their nutrient makeup—carbohydrate, protein, fat, and calories. This meal-planning system is called the food-choice system.

Starch. This group includes whole grains (brown rice, bulgur wheat, wheat berries, oats, barley), cereal, pasta, rice, breads, starchy vegetables (potatoes, corn, lima beans, and winter squashes such as acorn and spaghetti), crackers, desserts, and many snack-type foods.

Fruit. This group includes all varieties of fruit—fresh, frozen, canned, and dried—as well as fruit juices.

Milk. Included here are milk, yogurt, and buttermilk.

Nonstarchy Vegetables. The vegetable group is made up of nonstarchy vegetables, either raw or cooked, such as broccoli, asparagus, green beans, cabbage, carrots, salad greens, onions, tomatoes, and summer squashes like crookneck and zucchini. Starchy vegetables are included in the Starch group.

Meat and Meat Substitutes. This group includes beef, pork, lamb, veal, poultry, fish, seafood, eggs, tofu, cheese, cottage cheese, and peanut butter. Foods are then divided into lean, medium-fat, and high-fat choices.

Fat. You have obvious fats, like margarine, butter, cooking oils, mayonnaise, and salad dressings, plus other high-fat foods, like avocados, olives, nuts and seeds, bacon, sour cream, and cream cheese.

Using this system, if you want to adjust a menu, you can simply add or remove a serving (also called an exchange or food choice) of a certain food group, so the meal meets your needs. For a complete listing of the foods and serving sizes that compose a single exchange, purchase a copy of *Choose Your Foods: Food Lists for Diabetes*, available from the American Diabetes Association or The American Dietetic Association, or contact a registered dietitian.

CARBOHYDRATE COUNTING

The number of carbohydrate (carb) grams is listed on each menu. This will make it easy for you to count carbohydrates, if that's the method you use to follow a healthy meal plan.

Why should you count the grams of carb you eat? Because it is the carb in food that raises your blood glucose levels! And it raises them in predictable ways. If you eat about the same amount of carb at each meal and snack, there is a better chance that blood glucose levels will settle into a steady pattern, giving you more predictability and a much reduced risk of diabetes complications. You can also add new foods to your meal plan if you count the grams of carb in them—then you just substitute one carbohydrate-containing food for the other.

First, you need to know the number of carb grams in the food you're eating. If you're following the food choices meal planning system, each starch, fruit, and milk serving has about 15 grams of carbohydrate. A vegetable serving has about 5 grams of carbohydrate.

If you look at the Nutrition Facts on a food label, you'll find the carb grams per serving listed under Total Carbohydrate. (Be careful not to confuse the gram weight of the food, listed after the serving size, with grams of Total Carbohydrate.) Under Total Carbohydrate are Sugars and Dietary Fiber. Note that the Sugars are included in the Total Carb. Fiber is good, so you want to include more in your diet.

Next, you need to know how many grams of carb to eat at each meal, based on your diabetes treatment plan (exercise, diabetes pills, and/or insulin). Check with your health-care team to figure out how many carbs you should be eating every day.

It's important to measure your serving sizes. A bigger serving has more carb. Add up your carb totals at each meal, and try to keep your totals within your range to make managing your blood sugar a little bit easier.

HOW THIS BOOK HELPS

Simply check the carb gram total highlighted on each menu. To keep your daily totals consistent, choose meals and snacks that add up to your desired number. Knowing the carb totals for every meal really helps you stay consistent from day to day, but you still get to incorporate a variety of foods into your diet!

MENU TRACKER

	CALORIES	CARBS	FAT
BREAKFAST #			
ADJUSTMENTS			
Choice:			
Items changed:			
Meal Total:			
MORNING SNACK #			
LUNCH #			
ADJUSTMENTS			
Choice:			
Items changed:			
Meal Total:			
AFTERNOON SNACK #			
LUNCH #			
ADJUSTMENTS			
Choice:			
Items changed:			
Meal Total:			
EVENING SNACK #			
DAILY TOTAL:			

RECIPE CARDS

RECIPE PHOTOS ON PREVIOUS PAGE, CLOCKWISE FROM TOP LEFT:
Holiday Cranberry Rolls, pg. 194; Easy Spud Breakfast, pg. B34;
Old-fashioned Pot Roast and Gravy, pg. D20; Whole-wheat Pizza, pg. L41

RECIPE PHOTO ON PREVIOUS PAGE:

Peanut Butter and Jelly Muffins, pg. 106

SCONES

B41

SERVES: 16 • **SERVING SIZE:** 1 scone • **PREP TIME:** 25 minutes • **COOK TIME:** 7–10 minutes

3 tablespoons tub margarine (30–50% vegetable oil)
1 1/2 cups all-purpose flour
1/2 cup whole-wheat flour
1 1/2 teaspoons baking powder
1/2 teaspoon baking soda
1 packet sugar substitute
3/4 cup fat-free milk
1/4 cup dark raisins or currants
1/4 teaspoon grated orange peel
Nonstick cooking spray

1. Preheat oven to 450°F.
2. In food processor with fitted steel blade or a bowl with pastry blender, mix margarine and flours until it resembles coarse crumbs. Stir in baking powder, baking soda, sugar substitute, and add salt, if desired.
3. Stir in milk until dry ingredients are moistened. Stir in raisins and orange peel.
4. Gather dough into a ball. On a lightly floured surface, roll out dough to uniform 1/2-inch thickness. Cut into rounds using a 2 1/2-inch cookie cutter, or using a floured knife, cut the scones into triangles. Place on cookie sheet well sprayed with nonstick cooking spray.
5. Bake 7–10 minutes or until lightly browned.

CHOICES: 1 Starch	**CALORIES FROM FAT:** 10	**CHOLESTEROL:** 0 mg	**DIETARY FIBER:** 1 g
	TOTAL FAT: 1.0 g	**SODIUM:** 95 mg	**SUGARS:** 2 g
	SATURATED FAT: 0.2 g	**POTASSIUM:** 65 mg	**PROTEIN:** 2 g
CALORIES: 75	**TRANS FAT:** 0.0 g	**TOTAL CARBOHYDRATE:** 14 g	**PHOSPHORUS:** 85 mg

LOW COUNTRY GRITS AND SAUSAGE

B42

SERVES: 2 • **SERVING SIZE:** 1/2 loaf • **PREP TIME:** 10 minutes • **COOK TIME:** 1 hour + 15 minutes stand time

2 ounces turkey sausage
1/2 cup uncooked yellow or white grits (stone-ground are best)
2 large eggs, beaten
1/2 cup fat-free milk
1/2 teaspoon thyme
1/8 teaspoon garlic salt
Nonstick cooking spray

1. The night before: Sauté turkey sausage in a medium-hot pan and crumble into small pieces.
2. Cook grits according to package directions.
3. Combine eggs, milk, thyme, and garlic salt in a medium bowl. Add a small amount of hot grits and mix well. Add the rest of the grits and the sausage.
4. Mix well and pour into a loaf pan that has been coated with cooking spray. Cover and refrigerate overnight.
5. The next morning: Preheat oven to 350°F.
6. Remove grits mixture from refrigerator and let stand 15 minutes before baking. Bake for 40–45 minutes or until done.

CHOICES: 2 1/2 Starch, 1 Protein, medium fat	**CALORIES FROM FAT:** 65	**CHOLESTEROL:** 230 mg	**DIETARY FIBER:** 1 g
	TOTAL FAT: 7.0 g	**SODIUM:** 330 mg	**SUGARS:** 4 g
	SATURATED FAT: 2.2 g	**POTASSIUM:** 270 mg	**PROTEIN:** 18 g
CALORIES: 280	**TRANS FAT:** 0.1 g	**TOTAL CARBOHYDRATE:** 35 g	**PHOSPHORUS:** 230 mg

ENGLISH PANCAKES

SERVES: 4 • **SERVING SIZE:** 2 pancakes • **PREP TIME:** 10 minutes • **COOK TIME:** 5 minutes

1/2 cup all-purpose flour
1/2 cup whole-wheat flour
1 1/4 cups fat-free milk
2 egg whites
Nonstick cooking spray
1/2 cup fat-free cream cheese
8 teaspoons low-sugar jam
  or jelly

1 Combine flours, milk, and egg whites and beat until smooth.

2 Heat an 8- to 10-inch nonstick skillet that has been coated with cooking spray to medium-high. Put 1/4 cup batter into skillet and rotate skillet to spread batter evenly over bottom of pan. Cook for 20 seconds or until bubbles appear; flip and continue cooking for about another 20 seconds. (Treat pan with cooking spray between each pancake.) Place cooked pancakes on warm plate with waxed paper between them.

3 Microwave cheese until soft and spreadable (use low or defrost setting). Spread 1 tablespoon cheese and 1 teaspoon jam on each pancake and roll up.

CHOICES: 2 Starch, 1/2 Milk, fat-free	**CALORIES FROM FAT:** 0	**CHOLESTEROL:** 5 mg	**DIETARY FIBER:** 2 g
	TOTAL FAT: 0.0 g	**SODIUM:** 270 mg	**SUGARS:** 9 g
	SATURATED FAT: 0.1 g	**POTASSIUM:** 340 mg	**PROTEIN:** 12 g
CALORIES: 190	**TRANS FAT:** 0.0 g	**TOTAL CARBOHYDRATE:** 33 g	**PHOSPHORUS:** 325 mg

GRANOLA PANCAKES

B44

SERVES: 6 • **SERVING SIZE:** 3 (4-inch) pancakes • **PREP TIME:** 5 minutes • **COOK TIME:** 5 minutes

2 eggs or 1 egg and 2 egg whites
2 cups fat-free milk
2 tablespoons molasses
2 cups whole-wheat flour
1/2 cup low-fat granola
2 teaspoons baking powder
2 teaspoons artificial sweetener

1 Beat eggs in a large cup or bowl; add milk and molasses, and stir.

2 Combine remaining ingredients and mix into liquid mixture lightly with a fork.

3 Heat nonstick skillet over medium heat and cook pancakes using about 1/4 cup batter per pancake.

CHOICES: 2 1/2 Starch, 1/2 Milk, fat-free	**CALORIES FROM FAT:** 30	**CHOLESTEROL:** 70 mg	**DIETARY FIBER:** 6 g
	TOTAL FAT: 3.5 g	**SODIUM:** 185 mg	**SUGARS:** 12 g
	SATURATED FAT: 0.9 g	**POTASSIUM:** 460 mg	**PROTEIN:** 11 g
CALORIES: 255	**TRANS FAT:** 0.0 g	**TOTAL CARBOHYDRATE:** 47 g	**PHOSPHORUS:** 440 mg

ANGEL BISCUITS

ANGEL BISCUITS

ANGEL BISCUITS

SERVES: 36 • **SERVING SIZE:** 1 biscuit • **PREP TIME:** 15 minutes • **COOK TIME:** 12–15 minutes

B45

1 package quick-rising yeast
2 tablespoons warm water
2 cups all-purpose whole-wheat flour
3 cups all-purpose white flour
1 teaspoon baking soda
1 tablespoon baking powder
4 tablespoons sugar
2 teaspoons salt
1 cup shortening
2 cups low-fat buttermilk
Melted butter to brush tops (optional)
Nonstick butter-flavored cooking spray

1 Preheat oven to 400°F.
2 Dissolve yeast in lukewarm water.
3 Sift flour, baking soda, baking powder, sugar, and salt in a bowl. Cut in shortening, slowly mixing with a wooden spoon.
4 Add buttermilk and then yeast while slowly stirring mixture until all flour is dampened.
5 Knead on floured board for 1–2 minutes. Roll out to desired thickness and cut with a biscuit cutter. Dough may be refrigerated in an airtight container for several days to use as needed.
6 Spray cookie sheet with cooking spray and place biscuits on sheet.
7 If desired, brush with melted butter before or after baking. Bake about 12–15 minutes.

CHOICES: 1 Starch, 1 Fat
CALORIES: 122
CALORIES FROM FAT: 54
TOTAL FAT: 6.0 g
SATURATED FAT: 1.0 g
TRANS FAT: 0.0 g
CHOLESTEROL: 0 mg
SODIUM: 209 mg
POTASSIUM: 65 mg
TOTAL CARBOHYDRATE: 15 g
DIETARY FIBER: 1 g
SUGARS: 2 g
PROTEIN: 3 g
PHOSPHORUS: 85 mg

ATOMIC MUFFINS

SERVES: 24 • **SERVING SIZE:** 1 muffin • **PREP TIME:** 10 minutes • **COOK TIME:** 18 minutes

B46

1/2 cup canola or safflower oil
1/4 cup brown sugar
2 tablespoons molasses
2 eggs
3/4 cup fresh wheat germ
1 cup whole-wheat flour
1/4 cup soy flour
1/2 cup fat-free dry milk
1/2 cup ground sesame seeds
1/2 cup chopped sunflower seeds
1 1/2 cups low-fat milk or vanilla-flavored soy milk
2 teaspoons baking powder
1 cup raisins
1 cup chopped nuts
1/8 cup rolled oats
Nonstick cooking spray

1 Heat oven to 375°F. Mix the first 4 ingredients in a large mixing bowl. Add remaining ingredients and mix well.
2 Put paper cups in muffin tin or spray tin with nonstick cooking spray. Fill cups 2/3 full with batter. Bake 18 minutes.

CHOICES: 1 Carbohydrate, 1 Protein, lean, 1 1/2 Fat
CALORIES: 200
CALORIES FROM FAT: 110
TOTAL FAT: 12.0 g
SATURATED FAT: 1.5 g
TRANS FAT: 0.0 g
CHOLESTEROL: 20 mg
SODIUM: 55 mg
POTASSIUM: 280 mg
TOTAL CARBOHYDRATE: 19 g
DIETARY FIBER: 3 g
SUGARS: 9 g
PROTEIN: 6 g
PHOSPHORUS: 225 mg

BREAKFAST IN A COOKIE

SERVES: 13 • **SERVING SIZE:** 2 cookies • **PREP TIME:** 15 minutes • **COOK TIME:** 12–15 minutes

1/3 cup wheat bran or oat bran cereal
1/2 cup orange juice
1/4 cup sugar or honey
1/4 cup unsweetened applesauce
2 teaspoons vanilla
1 egg or 2 egg whites

1 cup whole-wheat pastry flour
1 teaspoon baking powder
1 teaspoon baking soda
1/3 cup fat-free dry milk
2 teaspoons fresh or bottled grated orange rind
2 teaspoons cinnamon

1 teaspoon nutmeg, optional
1 cup quick-cooking oats
1/2 cup finely chopped unsalted nuts
1 cup golden raisins
Nonstick cooking spray

1 Heat oven to 375°F.

2 In a small bowl, combine bran and orange juice; set aside. Mix honey, applesauce, vanilla, and eggs. Blend in bran-orange juice mix. Slowly blend the remaining ingredients into wet mixture until combined.

3 Drop by level tablespoons onto cookie sheets coated with cooking spray. Place about 2 inches apart. Bake 12–15 minutes or until golden brown.

CHOICES: 1/2 Starch, 1/2 Fruit	**CALORIES FROM FAT:** 20	**CHOLESTEROL:** 10 mg	**DIETARY FIBER:** 2 g
	TOTAL FAT: 2.0 g	**SODIUM:** 75 mg	**SUGARS:** 7 g
CALORIES: 85	**SATURATED FAT:** 0.3 g	**POTASSIUM:** 120 mg	**PROTEIN:** 2 g
	TRANS FAT: 0.0 g	**TOTAL CARBOHYDRATE:** 15 g	**PHOSPHORUS:** 80 mg

PEANUT BUTTER AND JELLY MUFFINS

SERVES: 12 • **SERVING SIZE:** 1 muffin • **PREP TIME:** 15 minutes • **COOK TIME:** 20–25 minutes

1 cup all-purpose flour
1 cup whole-wheat flour
3 tablespoons sugar
1 tablespoon baking powder
2/3 cup creamy peanut butter
1/4 cup egg substitute
1 cup fat-free milk
1/3 cup sugar-free jelly or preserves

1 Preheat oven to 350°F. Spray muffin tin with cooking spray or line with baking cups.

2 In a large bowl, mix flours, sugar, and baking powder.

3 In another bowl, beat peanut butter and egg substitute until smooth. Add milk a little at a time, stirring after each addition.

4 Pour peanut butter mixture over dry ingredients; fold in with a rubber spatula just until dry ingredients are moistened. Batter will be stiff.

5 Spoon 2 scant tablespoons batter into each muffin cup and smooth the surface out to the top edge of the cup. Then top each muffin with a heaping teaspoon jelly; cover with 2 more tablespoons of batter.

6 Bake 20–25 minutes or until lightly browned.

CHOICES: 2 Carbohydrate, 1 Protein, lean, 1/2 Fat	**CALORIES FROM FAT:** 70	**CHOLESTEROL:** 0 mg	**DIETARY FIBER:** 2 g
	TOTAL FAT: 8.0 g	**SODIUM:** 180 mg	**SUGARS:** 9 g
CALORIES: 200	**SATURATED FAT:** 1.6 g	**POTASSIUM:** 190 mg	**PROTEIN:** 7 g
	TRANS FAT: 0.0 g	**TOTAL CARBOHYDRATE:** 27 g	**PHOSPHORUS:** 235 mg

QUICK HOMEMADE RAISIN BREAD

SERVES: 18 • **SERVING SIZE:** 1/2–inch slice • **PREP TIME:** 40–45 minutes • **COOK TIME:** 40–45 minutes

3/4 cup dark seedless raisins

1 cup boiling water

Nonstick cooking spray

3/4 cup all-purpose flour

3/4 whole-wheat flour

1 teaspoon baking soda

7 packets artificial sweetener made with acesulfame-K or saccharin

1/2 teaspoon cinnamon

1/4 teaspoon salt

1 egg

1 teaspoon vanilla

1/4 cup canola oil

1 Combine raisins and boiling water; set aside for 30 minutes.

2 Preheat oven to 350°F. Spray a 9 × 5-inch loaf pan with cooking spray and lightly dust with flour.

3 In a large bowl, combine flours, baking soda, artificial sweetener, cinnamon, and salt.

4 In a small bowl, mix together egg, vanilla, oil, and raisins with liquid.

5 Add liquid ingredients to dry ingredients and mix until just moistened.

6 Pour into prepared loaf pan. Bake for 40–45 minutes or until golden brown and firm to the touch.

7 Let stand 5 minutes. Serve warm.

	CALORIES FROM FAT: 30	**CHOLESTEROL:** 10 mg	**DIETARY FIBER:** 1 g
	TOTAL FAT: 3.5 g	**SODIUM:** 105 mg	**SUGARS:** 4 g
CHOICES: 1 Starch, 1/2 Fat	**SATURATED FAT:** 0.3 g	**POTASSIUM:** 75 mg	**PROTEIN:** 2 g
CALORIES: 90	**TRANS FAT:** 0.0 g	**TOTAL CARBOHYDRATE:** 13 g	**PHOSPHORUS:** 35 mg

PORTOBELLO MUSHROOMS FLORENTINE

SERVES: 2 • **SERVING SIZE:** 1 portobello cap with spinach-egg mixture
PREP TIME: about 15 minutes • **COOK TIME:** about 15 minutes

2 portobello mushroom caps without stems, about 2 ounces each

1/2 teaspoon extra virgin olive oil

1/8 teaspoon fine sea salt

4 cups fresh baby spinach

2 large eggs

1 plum tomato sliced thinly

2 teaspoons grated Grana Padano or Parmigiano Reggiano cheese

1 Using a teaspoon, "wipe" the gills from the underside of the mushroom. Brush mushrooms with the extra virgin olive oil and sprinkle with the salt.

2 Heat a grill pan. Grill the mushrooms on the top side first, until you see grill marks. Turn and grill until they begin to soften.

3 Rinse the spinach even if the package says that it is washed. The water will help

to cook the spinach. Place the drained spinach in a medium sauté pan. Cook until spinach begins to wilt.

4 Divide spinach into two piles. Crack an egg over each pile. Cook until it begins to set and then turn the egg and spinach over to continue cooking the egg. Top the grilled portobello with this mixture. Top this with sliced tomatoes and sprinkle with cheese.

CHOICES: 1 Nonstarchy Vegetable, 1 Protein, medium fat, 1/2 Fat	**CALORIES FROM FAT:** 60	**CHOLESTEROL:** 185 mg	**DIETARY FIBER:** 2 g
	TOTAL FAT: 7.0 g	**SODIUM:** 280 mg	**SUGARS:** 2 g
	SATURATED FAT: 2.0 g	**POTASSIUM:** 720 mg	**PROTEIN:** 10 g
CALORIES: 120	**TRANS FAT:** 0.0 g	**TOTAL CARBOHYDRATE:** 6 g	**PHOSPHORUS:** 215 mg

EGGS BENEDICT WITH YOGURT HOLLANDAISE B51

SERVES: 4 • **SERVING SIZE:** 1/2 muffin + 1 egg + 1/2 ounce Canadian bacon + 3 tablespoons hollandaise sauce
PREP TIME: 10 minutes • **COOK TIME:** about 25 minutes

YOGURT HOLLANDAISE SAUCE:

1 tablespoon lemon juice
1/2 tablespoon melted butter
1/2 cup plain nonfat yogurt
1/8 teaspoon fine sea salt
1 egg

4 eggs
2 ounces Canadian bacon, cut into 4 slices
2 lite multigrain English muffins, split
1/2 cup baby spinach or arugula

1 Whisk all ingredients for the hollandaise in a saucepan. Heat to medium and whisk until mixture barely begins to boil. Remove from heat and cover to keep warm while preparing the eggs.

2 Bring a pan of water to a boil and reduce heat to simmer. Drop the eggs gently into the water. Cook to desired doneness.

3 Heat a nonstick skillet and cook the Canadian bacon.

4 Toast the English muffins.

5 Layer the English muffins, the spinach or arugula, the Canadian bacon, the eggs, and the hollandaise. Serve.

CHOICES: 1 Starch, 1 Protein, medium fat, 1/2 Fat
CALORIES: 190
CALORIES FROM FAT: 80
TOTAL FAT: 9.0 g
SATURATED FAT: 3.3 g
TRANS FAT: 0.1 g
CHOLESTEROL: 245 mg
SODIUM: 450 mg
POTASSIUM: 280 mg
TOTAL CARBOHYDRATE: 16 g
DIETARY FIBER: 4 g
SUGARS: 3 g
ADDED SUGARS: 0 g
PROTEIN: 15 g
PHOSPHORUS: 285 mg

WHOLE-WHEAT CURRANT SCONES B52

SERVES: 16 • **SERVING SIZE:** 1 scone • **PREP TIME:** 15 minutes • **COOK TIME:** 12–15 minutes

1 cup whole-wheat pastry flour
1 cup all-purpose white flour
1 cup quick-cooking oats
1/2 cup oat bran
2 tablespoons baking powder

1/4 teaspoon salt
1/4 teaspoon cream of tartar
4 tablespoons tub margarine, lower-fat spread (30–50% vegetable oil, trans fat–free)
1/2 cup currants

2/3 cup fat-free plain yogurt
1 tablespoon vanilla
1/4 cup orange juice
1/4 cup sugar
2 eggs

1 Heat oven to 425°F.

2 Mix first seven dry ingredients together in a large metal mixing bowl.

3 Cut in margarine until mixture resembles coarse meal.

4 In another bowl, combine remaining ingredients. Add to dry ingredients, mixing only until a ball of dough forms. If very dry, add 1–2 tablespoons more yogurt.

5 Knead dough on floured board about 10 times.

Divide in half and form two circles of dough about 1/2-inch thick.

6 Transfer to baking sheet and, with a wet knife, cut each circle into 8 pie-shaped wedges. Bake for 12–15 minutes.

CHOICES: 1 1/2 Starch, 1/2 Fat
CALORIES: 130
CALORIES FROM FAT: 26
TOTAL FAT: 3.0 g
SATURATED FAT: 1.0 g
TRANS FAT: 0.0 g
CHOLESTEROL: 27 mg
SODIUM: 209 mg
POTASSIUM: 130 mg
TOTAL CARBOHYDRATE: 22 g
DIETARY FIBER: 2 g
SUGARS: 5 g
PROTEIN: 5 g
PHOSPHORUS: 280 mg

RECIPE PHOTO ON PREVIOUS PAGE:
Ajiaco, pg. 114

WHOLE-WHEAT PIZZA

SERVES: 8 • **SERVING SIZE:** 1 slice • **PREP TIME:** 35 minutes • **COOK TIME:** 15–20 minutes

L41

1 cup warm water (110–115°F)
1 package (or 1 tablespoon) active dry yeast
1 tablespoon honey
2 cups whole-wheat flour, divided
1/2 teaspoon salt

3 ounces grated reduced-fat cheddar cheese
Fresh ground pepper
1/4 teaspoon garlic powder
1/2 cup unbleached white flour
1/2 cup water (if necessary)
1 tablespoon cornmeal

1/2 cup tomato or pizza sauce
1 tablespoon dried oregano
1 cup chopped broccoli
1 cup sliced mushrooms
1/2 cup shredded part-skim mozzarella cheese

1 Combine water, yeast, honey, and 1 cup of whole-wheat flour in a large bowl. Beat by hand for about 5 minutes or use the bread attachment of a mixer and beat for 5 minutes until mixture is smooth.

2 Let dough rise in a warm place for 15 minutes.

3 Preheat oven to 400°F. Add salt, cheddar cheese, pepper, garlic powder, remaining whole-wheat flour, and white flour to the dough. Add up to 1/2 cup water as needed to produce a smooth dough. Mix well and let the dough rest for about 5 minutes.

4 Pat dough evenly onto a baking sheet dusted with cornmeal, building up sides to form a crust. Top the dough with pizza sauce, oregano, vegetables, and cheese.

5 Bake pizza for 15–20 minutes until cheese melts and vegetables are cooked.

CHOICES: 2 Starch, 1 Protein, lean
CALORIES: 200
CALORIES FROM FAT: 40
TOTAL FAT: 3 g
SATURATED FAT: 1.4 g
TRANS FAT: 0.0 g
CHOLESTEROL: 10 mg
SODIUM: 350 mg
POTASSIUM: 280 mg
TOTAL CARBOHYDRATE: 34 g
DIETARY FIBER: 5 g
SUGARS: 4 g
PROTEIN: 11 g
PHOSPHORUS: 225 mg

HOPPIN' JOHN

SERVES: 8 • **SERVING SIZE:** 1 cup • **PREP TIME:** 5 minutes • **COOK TIME:** 1 hour 10 minutes

L42

1 cup raw cowpeas (dried field peas) or dried black-eyed peas
4 cups water
1 cup raw brown rice
4 slices bacon, fried crisp and fat drained
1 medium onion, chopped

1 Boil peas in lightly salted water until tender.

2 Add peas and 1 cup of the pea liquid to rice, bacon, and onion. Put in rice steamer or double boiler and cook for 1 hour or until rice is done.

CHOICES: 2 Starch, 1/2 Fat
CALORIES: 174
CALORIES FROM FAT: 23
TOTAL FAT: 3.0 g
SATURATED FAT: 1.0 g
TRANS FAT: 0.0 g
CHOLESTEROL: 3 mg
SODIUM: 52 mg
POTASSIUM: 270 mg
TOTAL CARBOHYDRATE: 31 g
DIETARY FIBER: 5 g
SUGARS: 3 g
PROTEIN: 7 g
PHOSPHORUS: 185 mg

CAESAR SALAD

SERVES: 4 • **SERVING SIZE:** 2 cups romaine + 3 tablespoons dressing + 1/2 tablespoon cheese + 1/2 cup croutons
PREP TIME: about 1 hour 15 minutes • **COOK TIME:** 5 minutes

1 medium head romaine lettuce

DRESSING

1 clove garlic, crushed

1/2 teaspoon black pepper

2 ounces smoked anchovies, drained and patted dry

1 egg yolk, hard boiled

1/4 cup lemon juice

2 tablespoons balsamic vinegar

1 teaspoon Dijon mustard

1 teaspoon Worcestershire sauce

1 1/2 tablespoons olive oil

CROUTONS

2 teaspoons olive oil

1 clove garlic, halved

4 1-ounce slices Italian bread (white or whole-wheat), cubed

1 tablespoon chopped parsley

2 tablespoons freshly grated Parmesan cheese

1. Crisp lettuce by separating leaves and rinsing well under cold water. Pat dry with paper towels and break into 2-inch pieces. Roll in clean paper towels and seal in plastic bag. Refrigerate until cold and crisp, about 1 hour.

2. For dressing, combine garlic, pepper, and anchovies in a blender. At high speed, blend until garlic and anchovies are finely chopped. Add egg yolk, lemon juice, vinegar, mustard, and Worcestershire sauce. Blend until mixture is smooth.

3. Turn blender on high and, with machine running, remove center of lid or lid itself. Slowly pour olive oil in a thin, steady stream. Blend until all oil is added and dressing is smooth and creamy. Set aside or refrigerate until ready to add to salad. Do not leave out of refrigeration for more than 1 hour.

4. For croutons, heat olive oil and garlic in medium skillet until oil is hot and garlic is fragrant. Remove pan from heat and cool to room temperature. Discard garlic.

5. Add the bread cubes and toss to coat. Sauté over medium-high heat until golden brown. Cool and cover with chopped parsley.

6. To build salad, place crisp lettuce pieces in a medium bowl. Pour dressing over salad and sprinkle with Parmesan cheese and croutons.

CHOICES: 1 Starch,
1 Nonstarchy Vegetable,
1 Protein, medium fat,
1 Fat
CALORIES: 210

CALORIES FROM FAT: 100
TOTAL FAT: 11.0 g
SATURATED FAT: 2.3 g
TRANS FAT: 0.0 g

CHOLESTEROL: 60 mg
SODIUM: 435 mg
POTASSIUM: 340 mg
TOTAL CARBOHYDRATE: 21 g

DIETARY FIBER: 3 g
SUGARS: 4 g
PROTEIN: 8 g
PHOSPHORUS: 105 mg

POTATOES WITH PEANUT SAUCE

L44

SERVES: 4 • **SERVING SIZE:** 1/2 cup potatoes + 1/4 cup sauce • **PREP TIME:** 10 minutes • **COOK TIME:** 12 minutes

1/2 cup roasted shelled peanuts
1/2 cup fat-free milk
1 teaspoon annatto oil
1/4 cup finely chopped white or yellow onion
1 clove garlic, minced

1 tablespoon finely chopped red bell pepper
1/2 cup low-fat, low-sodium chicken broth, homemade or canned
1/4 teaspoon salt
1/4 teaspoon ground white pepper

1 pound red potatoes, peeled, sliced or cubed, and cooked
Lettuce leaves
1 teaspoon chopped fresh cilantro, or to taste
5 teaspoons chopped peanuts

1 In a blender or food processor, blend peanuts and milk until smooth.

2 Heat oil in a nonstick skillet over medium-high heat. Sauté onion, garlic, and peppers for 1–2 minutes. Stir in chicken broth, peanut sauce, salt, and pepper.

3 Cook over medium-low heat until sauce thickens, about 8–10 minutes. Add the potatoes and toss gently.

4 Serve over lettuce leaves. Sprinkle each serving with cilantro and chopped peanuts.

CHOICES: 2 Starch, 2 Fat
CALORIES: 235

CALORIES FROM FAT: 110
TOTAL FAT: 12.0 g
SATURATED FAT: 1.7 g
TRANS FAT: 0.0 g

CHOLESTEROL: 0 mg
SODIUM: 195 mg
POTASSIUM: 550 mg
TOTAL CARBOHYDRATE: 26 g

DIETARY FIBER: 4 g
SUGARS: 4 g
PROTEIN: 8 g
PHOSPHORUS: 165 mg

CHICKEN RATATOUILLE

L45

SERVES: 4 • **SERVING SIZE:** 1 chicken breast half + 1 1/3 cups vegetables
PREP TIME: 10 minutes • **COOK TIME:** 20 minutes

4 skinless, boneless chicken breast halves
1 tablespoon olive oil
1 small eggplant, cubed
2 small zucchini, sliced

1 onion, sliced
1/2 pound mushrooms, sliced
1 green pepper, sliced
1 large tomato, seeded and cubed
1/2 teaspoon garlic powder

1 teaspoon dried parsley
1 teaspoon basil, or 1 tablespoon chopped fresh basil
Fresh ground pepper to taste
1/2 cup grated part-skim mozzarella cheese

1 Lightly salt chicken, if desired. Heat oil in large sauté pan. Sauté chicken about 2 minutes per side.

2 Add eggplant, zucchini, onion, mushrooms, and green pepper. Cover and cook 10 minutes.

3 Add tomato and remaining ingredients, except cheese. Simmer 3–5 minutes more.

4 Arrange chicken breasts on top of vegetables and sprinkle cheese over the chicken. Cook, uncovered, 1 more minute until cheese melts. Serve over barley or rice.

CHOICES: 3 Nonstarchy Vegetable, 4 Protein, lean, 1 Fat
CALORIES: 310

CALORIES FROM FAT: 90
TOTAL FAT: 10.0 g
SATURATED FAT: 3.0 g
TRANS FAT: 0.0 g

CHOLESTEROL: 95 mg
SODIUM: 175 mg
POTASSIUM: 920 mg
TOTAL CARBOHYDRATE: 18 g

DIETARY FIBER: 5 g
SUGARS: 8 g
PROTEIN: 39 g
PHOSPHORUS: 405 mg

COASTAL SANCOCHO

SERVES: 8 • **SERVING SIZE:** 1 cup • **PREP TIME:** 10 minutes • **COOK TIME:** 45 minutes

L46

1 tablespoon olive oil
1/2 onion, peeled and finely chopped
1 clove garlic, minced
1/4 cup finely chopped sweet or hot red pepper
1 tablespoon chopped cilantro
2 cups clam juice
4 cups water

1 pound cassava (yucca), peeled and cut into 4 pieces
1 tablespoon fat-free milk
2 medium potatoes, peeled and cut into chunks
2 medium carrots, cubed
1/2 ripe plantain, cut into 1-inch pieces
1/2 pound firm-fleshed white fish

(halibut, sea bass, or cod), cut into bite-sized pieces
1/2 pound fillet of sole, cut into bite-sized pieces
1/2 teaspoon fresh lime juice
1/2 cup fresh or frozen peas
1/2 cup finely chopped cabbage
1/2 cup chopped white onion
1/2 cup chopped cilantro

1 Heat oil in large stockpot and sauté onion, garlic, peppers, and cilantro for 3–4 minutes. Add clam juice and water and bring to a boil.

2 Add cassava and milk, cover, and simmer for 20 minutes.

3 Add potatoes, carrots, plantain, fish, and lime juice and simmer for 15 minutes. Add peas and

cabbage and simmer 5 minutes.

4 Combine onion and cilantro in small bowl. Garnish each soup serving with 1 tablespoon mixture.

CHOICES: 2 Starch, 1 Protein, lean
CALORIES: 206
CALORIES FROM FAT: 25

TOTAL FAT: 3 g
SATURATED FAT: 0.0 g
TRANS FAT: 0.0 g
CHOLESTEROL: 26 mg

SODIUM: 194 mg
POTASSIUM: 650 mg
TOTAL CARBOHYDRATE: 32 g
DIETARY FIBER: 3 g

SUGARS: 6 g
PROTEIN: 14 g
PHOSPHORUS: 240 mg
PROTEIN: 14 g

AJIACO

SERVES: 9 • **SERVING SIZE:** 1 cup • **PREP TIME:** 10 minutes • **COOK TIME:** 55 minutes

L47

2 tablespoons canola oil, divided
1 1/2 pounds beef stew meat
4 cups low-fat, low-sodium beef broth
2 cups water
1 large onion, peeled and cut into thin vertical slices

8 medium potatoes, peeled and quartered
2 large carrots, julienned
1 cup chard, washed and chopped
1–2 cloves garlic, minced
1/2 teaspoon oregano

1 teaspoon salt
1/4 teaspoon black pepper
1/2 cup chopped celery
1 tablespoon chopped parsley
Hot pepper sauce to taste
2 hard-boiled eggs, sliced

1 Heat 1 tablespoon oil in large stockpot and brown meat 4–5 minutes. Add broth and water and bring to a boil. Cover, reduce heat, and simmer 30 minutes.

2 Heat remaining 1 tablespoon oil in small skillet and brown onion.

3 Add to stockpot, along with remaining ingredients

except hot sauce and egg. Simmer for 20 minutes.

3 Season with hot sauce and place egg slice in each bowl before serving.

CHOICES: 1 1/2 Starch, 2 Protein, lean, 1 Nonstarchy Vegetable
CALORIES: 230

CALORIES FROM FAT: 74
TOTAL FAT: 7 g
SATURATED FAT: 1.6 g
TRANS FAT: 0.0 g

CHOLESTEROL: 75 mg
SODIUM: 380 mg
POTASSIUM: 700 mg
TOTAL CARBOHYDRATE: 26 g

DIETARY FIBER: 3 g
SUGARS: 3 g
PROTEIN: 17 g
PHOSPHORUS: 195 mg

TUSCAN CHICKEN SOUP

SERVES: 10 • **SERVING SIZE:** 1 cup • **PREP TIME:** 5 minutes • **COOK TIME:** 25 minutes

L48

1 pound boneless, skinless, chicken breast

1 tablespoon extra virgin olive oil

1 cup chopped onion, about 1 large onion

1 tablespoon minced garlic, about 3 medium cloves

1 cup sliced celery, about 2 stalks

1 cup sliced carrots, about 2 medium carrots

2 cups sliced zucchini, about 1 medium zucchini

1 cup grape tomatoes

2 1/2 cups cannellini beans (2 15-ounce cans, drained and rinsed)

1 tablespoon chopped fresh rosemary

1/4 cup fresh basil leaves, torn

1 teaspoon fine sea salt

1/2 teaspoon freshly ground black pepper

48 ounces low-sodium, low-fat chicken stock

1 Cut chicken breast into bite-sized pieces.

2 Place olive oil, onion, garlic, and chicken breast in 6- or 8-quart soup pot.

3 Sauté until onions become translucent. Add celery, carrots, zucchini, and tomatoes and cook 5 minutes.

4 Add beans, herbs, and stock. Bring to a boil, reduce heat to just above a boil and cook 20 minutes.

CHOICES: 1/2 Starch, 1 Nonstarchy Vegetable, 2 Protein, lean
CALORIES: 160

CALORIES FROM FAT: 30
TOTAL FAT: 3.5 g
SATURATED FAT: 0.9 g
TRANS FAT: 0.0 g

CHOLESTEROL: 25 mg
SODIUM: 380 mg
POTASSIUM: 570 mg
TOTAL CARBOHYDRATE: 15 g

DIETARY FIBER: 4 g
SUGARS: 2 g
PROTEIN: 17 g
PHOSPHORUS: 175 mg

CARIBBEAN CHICKEN STEW

SERVES: 8 • **SERVING SIZE:** 1 cup stew + 1 piece chicken • **PREP TIME:** 10 minutes + 1 hour • **COOK TIME:** 45 minutes

L49

2 tablespoons olive oil

2–3 cloves garlic, minced

1/4 teaspoon oregano

Dash paprika

1/4 teaspoon salt

Dash black pepper

3-pound chicken, cut into 8 pieces, skin and fat removed

2 teaspoons canola oil

1/8 teaspoon annatto (achiote) powder

2 tablespoons *Sofrito* (page 166)

1/2 cup tomato sauce

2 cups low-fat, low-sodium chicken broth

2 cups water

2 cups uncooked long-grain brown rice

1 cup frozen peas

2 tablespoons pimiento (optional)

1 Combine olive oil, garlic, oregano, paprika, salt, and pepper in large container. Add chicken and refrigerate for at least 1 hour.

2 Heat oil in large stockpot. Add annatto and stir until oil turns bright orange. Sauté sofrito for 2–3 minutes. Add chicken and sauté 5–6 minutes. Add tomato sauce, reduce heat, cover, and cook for 10–15 minutes. Stir several times.

3 Add chicken broth and water and bring to a boil. Reduce heat, add rice, cover, and cook 15 minutes. Add peas, cover, and cook 3 more minutes. Garnish with pimiento, if desired.

CHOICES: 2 1/2 Starch, 2 Protein, lean, 1/2 Fat
CALORIES: 340

CALORIES FROM FAT: 90
TOTAL FAT: 10.0 g
SATURATED FAT: 2.0 g
TRANS FAT: 0.0 g

CHOLESTEROL: 50 mg
SODIUM: 240 mg
POTASSIUM: 370 mg
TOTAL CARBOHYDRATE: 39 g

DIETARY FIBER: 3 g
SUGARS: 2 g
PROTEIN: 21 g
PHOSPHORUS: 285 mg

MIXED GREENS WITH ORANGE VINAIGRETTE

L50

SERVES: 8 • **SERVING SIZE:** 1 cup + 1 1/2 tablespoons dressing • **PREP TIME:** 10 minutes • **CHILL TIME:** 1 hour

1/4 cup white wine vinegar
1/4 cup orange juice
2 packets artificial sweetener
2 tablespoons finely chopped onion
2 teaspoons extra-virgin olive oil
2 teaspoons Dijon mustard
3 cups torn iceberg lettuce

3 cups torn spinach leaves
2 cups cubed lean cooked ham
1 cup halved seedless red grapes
1/4 cup sliced green onions
11-ounce can mandarin orange segments, chilled and drained

1 In a blender or jar with a tight-fitting lid, combine first six ingredients, add salt and pepper, if desired, and shake well. Refrigerate 1 hour.

2 In a large bowl, combine remaining ingredients. Pour dressing over mixture and toss gently.

CHOICES: 1 Protein, lean, 1/2 Fruit
CALORIES: 99

CALORIES FROM FAT: 29
TOTAL FAT: 3.0 g
SATURATED FAT: 1.0 g
TRANS FAT: 0.0 g

CHOLESTEROL: 20 mg
SODIUM: 508 mg
POTASSIUM: 300 mg
TOTAL CARBOHYDRATE: 8 g

DIETARY FIBER: 1 g
SUGARS: 6 g
PROTEIN: 10 g
PHOSPHORUS: 100 mg

NUTTY RICE LOAF

L51

SERVES: 6 • **SERVING SIZE:** 1 slice • **PREP TIME:** 5 minutes • **COOK TIME:** 40–45 minutes + 5 minutes stand time

Nonstick cooking spray
1 1/2 cups cooked brown rice
1 cup shredded zucchini
1/4 cup chopped onion
1/2 cup wheat germ
1/4 cup chopped walnuts
1 cup shredded fat-free cheddar cheese
2 eggs
1/4 cup egg substitute
1 teaspoon thyme
1 teaspoon marjoram

1 Preheat oven to 350°F. Spray a 9 × 5-inch loaf pan with nonstick cooking spray. Combine all ingredients in a mixing bowl until mixture has the consistency of wet dough. Add salt and pepper, if desired.

2 Pack into loaf pan. Bake for 40–45 minutes until browned. Edges will pull back from the sides of the pan. Remove from oven and let cool for 5 minutes before slicing.

CHOICES: 1 Starch, 2 Protein, lean, 1/2 Fat
CALORIES: 190

CALORIES FROM FAT: 55
TOTAL FAT: 6.0 g
SATURATED FAT: 1.1 g
TRANS FAT: 0.0 g

CHOLESTEROL: 75 mg
SODIUM: 235 mg
POTASSIUM: 270 mg
TOTAL CARBOHYDRATE: 19 g

DIETARY FIBER: 3 g
SUGARS: 2 g
PROTEIN: 14 g
PHOSPHORUS: 310 mg

STUFFED PEPPERS

L52

SERVES: 4 • **SERVING SIZE:** 1 pepper • **PREP TIME:** 10 minutes • **COOK TIME:** 25 minutes

1 tablespoon canola oil
2 tablespoons *Sofrito* (page 166)
1 pound 96% lean ground beef
1/4 cup tomato sauce

1 tablespoon tomato paste
4 medium green or red bell peppers
1/4 cup water

1/2 cup shredded fat-free cheese (mozzarella, muenster, jack, asadero, or cheddar)

1 Heat oil in a medium skillet over medium-high heat. Add sofrito and sauté 3–4 minutes. Add meat and brown 5–6 minutes. Stir in tomato sauce and paste. Reduce heat, cover, and cook for 10 minutes.

2 Meanwhile, wash peppers. With a small knife, carefully cut a small circle around the stem area. Lift the stem and seeds out. Rinse peppers to remove any remaining seeds.

3 Place peppers in a 3-inch-deep microwave-safe dish next to each other so they support each other standing.

4 Add water and cover. Cook at high power for 2–3 minutes or until the peppers are slightly soft. Remove from the microwave and drain. Careful—the peppers will be hot!

5 With a soup spoon, fill peppers with filling. Cover the opening of each pepper with 2 tablespoons grated cheese. Place stuffed peppers back in dish. Cover and microwave 4–5 minutes.

CHOICES: 2 Nonstarchy Vegetable, 4 Protein, lean	**CALORIES FROM FAT:** 90	**CHOLESTEROL:** 70 mg	**DIETARY FIBER:** 2 g
	TOTAL FAT: 9.0 g	**SODIUM:** 320 mg	**SUGARS:** 6 g
	SATURATED FAT: 2.4 g	**POTASSIUM:** 710 mg	**PROTEIN:** 32 g
CALORIES: 250	**TRANS FAT:** 0.2 g	**TOTAL CARBOHYDRATE:** 11 g	**PHOSPHORUS:** 325 mg

TOFU-VEGETABLE STIR-FRY

L53

SERVES: 4 • **SERVING SIZE:** 2 cups • **PREP TIME:** 10 minutes • **COOK TIME:** 15 minutes

1/2 pound firm tofu, cubed
2 tablespoons olive oil
1 cup carrots, sliced diagonally
2 cups chopped broccoli

1 cup sliced bell pepper
1/2 cup chopped onion
2 teaspoon basil
1 cup sliced mushrooms

1 1/2 tablespoons chopped garlic
2 tablespoons light soy sauce or tamari
1/4 cup sesame seeds

1 Sauté tofu in oil. Flip cubes once or twice to brown on a few sides, about 5 minutes.

2 Add carrots and mix; then add broccoli, peppers, onions, basil, mushrooms, and garlic. Sauté about 5–7 minutes, until soft.

3 Turn off heat, add soy sauce, and cover. Let steam for a minute or two before serving. Top with sesame seeds. Serve with rice or noodles.

CHOICES: 2 Nonstarchy Vegetable, 1 Protein, medium fat, 1 1/2 Fat	**CALORIES FROM FAT:** 115	**CHOLESTEROL:** 0 mg	**DIETARY FIBER:** 4 g
	TOTAL FAT: 13.0 g	**SODIUM:** 340 mg	**SUGARS:** 5 g
	SATURATED FAT: 1.9 g	**POTASSIUM:** 520 mg	**PROTEIN:** 9 g
CALORIES: 195	**TRANS FAT:** 0.0 g	**TOTAL CARBOHYDRATE:** 13 g	**PHOSPHORUS:** 180 mg

TAMALES

SERVES: 4 • **SERVING SIZE:** 2 corn dumplings • **PREP TIME:** 30 minutes • **COOK TIME:** 50 minutes

3 small ears fresh corn or
   2 cups frozen corn, thawed

Corn husks, fresh or dried and
   soaked

1 tablespoon fat-free milk
   (optional)

2 teaspoons canola oil

1 teaspoon tub margarine
   (60–70% vegetable oil, no
   trans fat)

2 tablespoons grated onion

1 clove garlic, minced

2 tablespoons reduced-fat
   grated Parmesan cheese

1/4 teaspoon salt

1 teaspoon baking powder

1 egg, beaten

1. Carefully remove corn husks from fresh corn. Clean and set aside until needed. If you use frozen corn, use dried corn husks that have been soaked for several hours or overnight. Remove husks from water, drain, and dry with a clean paper towel.

2. Remove the corn from the cob. Set aside the cobs. In a blender or food processor, blend the corn until it forms a soft dough. Add milk if needed to process the mixture.

3. Heat oil and margarine in a medium skillet over medium heat. Sauté onion and garlic for 2 minutes. Add corn and stir. Pour into a large bowl.

4. In a small bowl, mix together cheese, salt, and baking powder. Stir into corn mixture. Add egg and beat until dough is smooth and of uniform consistency. The dough should be slightly soft. If needed, adjust consistency with fat-free milk.

5. Place 2 corn husks in opposite directions, the wide part of one on top of the other, creating a rectangular zone in the center. In this area, place 2 tablespoons corn mixture. Carefully fold 1 husk toward the center, then the other. Repeat. The husks should cover the mixture completely, including the sides. Tie packets with strips of corn husks or with string, if necessary.

6. Steam 45 minutes in a bamboo steamer over boiling water. If you don't have a bamboo steamer, place corn cobs on the bottom of a large pot. Add 2–3 inches of water, bring to a gentle boil, and place packets on the cobs sealed side down. Cover and steam 45 minutes.

7. Unwrap and serve.

CHOICES: 1 Starch, 1 Fat
CALORIES: 135

CALORIES FROM FAT: 55
TOTAL FAT: 6.0 g
SATURATED FAT: 1.2 g
TRANS FAT: 0.0 g

CHOLESTEROL: 55 mg
SODIUM: 325 mg
POTASSIUM: 190 mg
TOTAL CARBOHYDRATE: 20 g

DIETARY FIBER: 2 g
SUGARS: 3 g
PROTEIN: 5 g
PHOSPHORUS: 220 mg

RECIPE PHOTO ON PREVIOUS PAGE:

Meat and Vegetable Empanadas, pg. 136

CRAB CAKE

SERVES: 4 • **SERVING SIZE:** 1 crab cake • **PREP TIME:** 15 minutes • **COOK TIME:** 20 minutes

Nonstick cooking spray
1/2 pound lump crabmeat, flaked
1 tablespoon Dijon mustard
1 tablespoon tub margarine
 (30–50% vegetable oil, trans
 fat–free), melted
1 egg, lightly beaten
2 teaspoons lemon juice
1 teaspoon Worcestershire sauce
Pinch cayenne pepper
2 dashes Tabasco sauce
1/2 cup soft bread crumbs
Lemon wedges

1 Preheat oven to 400°F. Spray baking sheet with nonstick cooking spray.

2 Combine crabmeat, mustard, margarine, egg, lemon juice, Worcestershire sauce, cayenne pepper, and Tabasco sauce. Add 2–4 tablespoons bread crumbs to bind mixture.

3 Shape into 4 cakes. Roll in remaining bread crumbs; place on prepared cookie sheet.

4 Bake for 20 minutes, until crab cakes are lightly browned, turning the crab cakes over once. Add salt and pepper, if desired. Serve with lemon wedges, if desired.

CHOICES: 2 Protein, lean
CALORIES: 100

CALORIES FROM FAT: 30
TOTAL FAT: 3.5 g
SATURATED FAT: 0.8 g
TRANS FAT: 0.0 g

CHOLESTEROL: 130 mg
SODIUM: 340 mg
POTASSIUM: 230 mg
TOTAL CARBOHYDRATE: 4 g

DIETARY FIBER: 0 g
SUGARS: 1 g
PROTEIN: 12 g
PHOSPHORUS: 165 mg

LEMON BARBECUED CHICKEN

D42

SERVES: 2 • **SERVING SIZE:** 3 ounces chicken
PREP TIME: 20 minutes + 2 hours chill time • **COOK TIME:** 15 minutes

1/2 teaspoon grated lemon rind
1/2 teaspoon salt
1/4 teaspoon dry mustard
1/4 teaspoon dried oregano
1/4 cup lemon juice
1/4 cup canola oil
1 tablespoon chopped
 green onion
1/2 teaspoon Worcestershire
 sauce
1/2 pound boneless, skinless
 chicken breasts

1 Mix together all ingredients except chicken. Pour mixture over chicken in large glass or stainless steel bowl; marinate in refrigerator for 2 hours.

2 Remove chicken from refrigerator and let stand for 15 minutes to ensure that the chicken will cook evenly. Prepare an oven

broiler or grill; if grilling, spray the rack thoroughly with nonstick cooking spray.

3 Remove chicken from marinade. Discard leftover marinade. Broil or grill 6 inches from the heat source, turning once for a total of 15 minutes or until chicken is tender and no trace of pink remains.

CHOICES: 3 Protein, lean,
 1 Fat
CALORIES: 190

CALORIES FROM FAT: 90
TOTAL FAT: 10.0 g
SATURATED FAT: 1.3 g
TRANS FAT: 0.0 g

CHOLESTEROL: 65 mg
SODIUM: 215 mg
POTASSIUM: 210 mg
TOTAL CARBOHYDRATE: 1 g

DIETARY FIBER: 0 g
SUGARS: 0 g
PROTEIN: 24 g
PHOSPHORUS: 180 mg

SHISH KABOB

SERVES: 4 • **SERVING SIZE:** 1 skewer • **PREP TIME:** 25 minutes + 2 hour marinate time • **COOK TIME:** 10 minutes

4 wooden skewers
1 pound boneless sirloin
1/2 cup vinegar (balsamic, red wine, white wine, herb)
2 tablespoons canola oil
1 medium onion, chopped
2 tablespoons minced fresh parsley
1 green pepper, cut into 2-inch squares
6 small tomatoes, halved

1 Soak skewers in warm water for 15 minutes (prevents them from burning on the grill).
2 Trim fat from meat and cut into 1 1/2-inch cubes.
3 Mix vinegar, oil, onion, and parsley. Add pepper and salt to mixture, if desired. Add steak. Cover and marinate in the refrigerator for 2 hours, stirring occasionally.

4 Remove meat from the marinade and remove skewers from water. Alternate meat on skewers with green pepper and tomatoes. Brush with marinade.
5 Prepare an oven broiler or grill. Broil or grill 4 inches from the heat source for a total of 10 minutes, turning once.

CHOICES: 2 Nonstarchy Vegetable, 3 Protein, lean, 1 1/2 Fat
CALORIES: 250

CALORIES FROM FAT: 110
TOTAL FAT: 12.0 g
SATURATED FAT: 2.2 g
TRANS FAT: 0.2 g

CHOLESTEROL: 40 mg
SODIUM: 60 mg
POTASSIUM: 760 mg
TOTAL CARBOHYDRATE: 11 g

DIETARY FIBER: 3 g
SUGARS: 6 g
PROTEIN: 24 g
PHOSPHORUS: 235 mg

SPINACH-STUFFED CHICKEN BREASTS

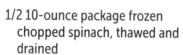

SERVES: 4 • **SERVING SIZE:** 3 ounces chicken + 3 tablespoons stuffing
PREP TIME: 10 minutes • **COOK TIME:** 45–50 minutes

1/2 10-ounce package frozen chopped spinach, thawed and drained
1/4 cup fat-free ricotta cheese
3 tablespoons shredded part-skim mozzarella cheese
1/4 teaspoon tarragon
2 whole chicken breasts (about 1 1/2 pounds total), halved and boned (leave skin on)
1/2 teaspoon tub margarine, melted

1 Preheat oven to 350°F.
2 Combine spinach, cheeses, and tarragon. Add salt and pepper, if desired.
3 Lift up skin of each chicken breast and divide mixture evenly among them. Be careful not to tear skin. Smooth skin over stuffing; tuck underneath to form a neat package.

4 Brush each breast with melted margarine. Place in 2-quart baking dish.
5 Bake uncovered for 45–50 minutes until chicken is browned and no trace of pink remains.
6 Remove and discard skin after cooking.

CHOICES: 4 Protein, lean
CALORIES: 175

CALORIES FROM FAT: 35
TOTAL FAT: 4.0 g
SATURATED FAT: 1.4 g
TRANS FAT: 0.0 g

CHOLESTEROL: 80 mg
SODIUM: 135 mg
POTASSIUM: 320 mg
TOTAL CARBOHYDRATE: 2 g

DIETARY FIBER: 1 g
SUGARS: 1 g
PROTEIN: 31 g
PHOSPHORUS: 260 mg

SALLY'S HAWAIIAN CHICKEN

SERVES: 8 • **SERVING SIZE:** 3 ounces chicken + 1/2 cup vegetable-fruit mixture
PREP TIME: 5 minutes • **COOK TIME:** 1 hour

2 pounds boneless, skinless chicken breasts

1/2 cup low-sodium, low-fat chicken broth

1/2 cup chopped green pepper

1 medium onion, chopped

1 cup sliced fresh mushrooms

20-ounce can unsweetened chunk pineapple, juice reserved

1/2 cup water

2 tablespoons lite soy sauce

2 teaspoons instant granulated chicken bouillon

1/2 teaspoon ground ginger

1 Preheat oven to 350°F. In a large nonstick ovenproof skillet over medium-high heat, brown the chicken in broth on both sides for a total of 5–7 minutes.

2 Add green pepper and onion and cook for 5 minutes. Add remaining ingredients, including reserved pineapple juice. Add salt and pepper, if desired.

3 Transfer skillet to the oven and bake uncovered for 40–45 minutes until chicken is tender and no trace of pink remains.

CHOICES: 1/2 Fruit, 1 Nonstarchy Vegetable, 3 Protein, lean
CALORIES: 180
CALORIES FROM FAT: 25
TOTAL FAT: 3.0 g
SATURATED FAT: 0.8 g
TRANS FAT: 0.0 g
CHOLESTEROL: 65 mg
SODIUM: 435 mg
POTASSIUM: 370 mg
TOTAL CARBOHYDRATE: 12 g
DIETARY FIBER: 2 g
SUGARS: 9 g
PROTEIN: 26 g
PHOSPHORUS: 210 mg

TOMATOED FISH FILLETS

SERVES: 4 • **SERVING SIZE:** 1 fillet • **PREP TIME:** 10 minutes • **COOK TIME:** 30 minutes

1 pound frozen cod fillets, cut into 4 pieces

1/2 teaspoon thyme

1/2 10.75-ounce can lower-fat, lower-sodium cream of mushroom soup

1 medium tomato, sliced

1 teaspoon tub margarine (30–50% vegetable oil, trans fat–free, melted)

1/2 teaspoon dried dill weed

1 Preheat oven to 350°F. Place fish fillets in ungreased baking dish. Stir thyme into soup; spoon over fish. Bake uncovered for 25 minutes. Remove from oven.

2 Place 1 slice tomato on each fillet. Brush tomato with margarine and sprinkle with dill weed. Return fish to oven and bake 5 minutes longer, until fish flakes easily with fork.

CHOICES: 3 Protein, lean
CALORIES: 125
CALORIES FROM FAT: 20
TOTAL FAT: 2.0 g
SATURATED FAT: 0.4 g
TRANS FAT: 0.0 g
CHOLESTEROL: 50 mg
SODIUM: 205 mg
POTASSIUM: 560 mg
TOTAL CARBOHYDRATE: 5 g
DIETARY FIBER: 1 g
SUGARS: 2 g
PROTEIN: 21 g
PHOSPHORUS: 145 mg

HURRY-UP BEEF STEW

D47

SERVES: 4 • **SERVING SIZE:** 1 1/2 cups • **PREP TIME:** 10 minutes • **COOK TIME:** 40 minutes

1 tablespoon canola oil

1 pound lean top sirloin steak, trimmed of fat and cut into thin strips

1 small onion, halved and cut into thin strips

2 celery stalks, sliced

2 carrots, thinly sliced

4 small new potatoes, halved

10.75-ounce can light cream of mushroom soup

1/3 cup water

1 bay leaf

1 teaspoon dried parsley

1/4 teaspoon thyme

1. Heat oil in large heavy pan or Dutch oven until very hot. Add steak strips and quickly brown on all sides. Remove from pan and place in a bowl.

2. Place onion, celery, and carrots into pan and quickly sauté. Add potatoes and reserved browned meat, with juices.

3. Add mushroom soup, water, and seasonings and stir until mixed.

4. Cover, reduce heat to simmer, and cook for about 30 minutes, or until meat and potatoes are tender. Remove bay leaf and serve.

CHOICES: 1 1/2 Starch, 1 Nonstarchy Vegetable, 3 Protein, lean, 1/2 Fat
CALORIES: 305

CALORIES FROM FAT: 80
TOTAL FAT: 9.0 g
SATURATED FAT: 2.2 g
TRANS FAT: 0.2 g

CHOLESTEROL: 45 mg
SODIUM: 355 mg
POTASSIUM: 1250 mg
TOTAL CARBOHYDRATE: 29 g

DIETARY FIBER: 4 g
SUGARS: 5 g
PROTEIN: 26 g
PHOSPHORUS: 260 mg

SMOTHERED CHICKEN

D48

SERVES: 4 • **SERVING SIZE:** 1 leg or 1/2 breast + 1/2 cup vegetables
PREP TIME: 10 minutes • **COOK TIME:** 55 minutes

3 pieces chicken, skin removed (2 legs and 1 breast)

1 tablespoon canola oil

1 large onion, sliced

2 cloves garlic, crushed

1/2 teaspoon crushed thyme

2 cups water

1 1/2 cups carrots, sliced

1 1/2 cups frozen peas

1. Lightly salt and pepper the chicken, if desired.

2. In a deep saucepan or Dutch oven, heat oil until hot. Add chicken and brown quickly on both sides. Turn off heat and pour off excess oil.

3. Add onion, garlic, and thyme to chicken.

4. Cover chicken with water. Bring to a boil. Lower heat, cover pot, and simmer for about 20 minutes.

5. Add carrots and peas to chicken. Cover and simmer for 30 minutes more.

CHOICES: 1/2 Starch, 2 Nonstarchy Vegetable, 4 Protein, lean, 1/2 Fat
CALORIES: 285

CALORIES FROM FAT: 90
TOTAL FAT: 10.0 g
SATURATED FAT: 1.9 g
TRANS FAT: 0.0 g

CHOLESTEROL: 90 mg
SODIUM: 150 mg
POTASSIUM: 540 mg
TOTAL CARBOHYDRATE: 17 g

DIETARY FIBER: 5 g
SUGARS: 7 g
PROTEIN: 32 g
PHOSPHORUS: 280 mg

MIKE'S VEAL

SERVES: 4 • **SERVING SIZE:** 4 ounces veal + 1/2 cup vegetables • **PREP TIME:** 10 minutes • **COOK TIME:** 15 minutes

1 pound veal scaloppine
(already pounded thin)
1/4 cup whole-wheat flour
1 tablespoon olive oil
1/2 cup wine (red or white)
2 cloves garlic, minced
8 ounce fresh mushrooms,
thinly sliced
4 Roma tomatoes, seeded
and diced

1 Dust veal lightly with flour.
2 Heat heavy skillet to
medium-high and add oil.
When oil is hot, add veal
and quickly cook until lightly
browned on both sides.
3 Remove veal and add
wine to pan (to deglaze).
Cook until almost dry
and then add garlic and
mushrooms. Cook, stirring,
about 2 minutes, or until
mushrooms are tender.
4 Add tomatoes and
reserved veal. Cover and
heat 2 minutes. Serve
immediately.

CHOICES: 1/2 Starch,
1 Nonstarchy Vegetable,
3 Protein, lean, 1/2 Fat
CALORIES: 220

CALORIES FROM FAT: 65
TOTAL FAT: 7.0 g
SATURATED FAT: 1.5 g
TRANS FAT: 0.0 g

CHOLESTEROL: 75 mg
SODIUM: 65 mg
POTASSIUM: 690 mg
TOTAL CARBOHYDRATE: 10 g

DIETARY FIBER: 2 g
SUGARS: 3 g
PROTEIN: 27 g
PHOSPHORUS: 305 mg

NEW ENGLAND CHICKEN CROQUETTES

SERVES: 4 • **SERVING SIZE:** 2 croquettes
PREP TIME: 10 minutes + 20 minutes chill time • **COOK TIME:** 35 minutes

2 tablespoons tub margarine
(60–70% vegetable oil, no
trans fat)
2 tablespoons flour
1 cup fat-free milk
1 teaspoon Worcestershire sauce
1/2 teaspoon chervil
1/4 teaspoon salt
1/8 teaspoon white pepper
2 cups cooked chicken breast,
finely chopped or shredded
in food processor
1 tablespoon water
1/2 cup egg substitute
2/3 cup bread crumbs
Nonstick cooking spray

1 Preheat oven to 375°F.
2 Melt margarine over
low heat; stir in flour
until smooth. Add milk
gradually, whisk until
smooth; add Worcestershire
sauce, chervil, salt, pepper,
and chicken. Cool in
refrigerator until easy to
work with.
3 Make egg wash by mixing
water with egg substitute.
Set aside.
4 When chicken mixture is
cool, form into 8 balls using
1/3 cup mixture per ball.
5 Roll in bread crumbs, egg
wash, and again in bread
crumbs.
6 Place on cookie sheet well
sprayed with cooking spray.
Bake 20–25 minutes until
light golden brown.

CHOICES: 1 1/2 Starch,
3 Protein, lean
CALORIES: 275

CALORIES FROM FAT: 70
TOTAL FAT: 8.0 g
SATURATED FAT: 1.9 g
TRANS FAT: 0.0 g

CHOLESTEROL: 60 mg
SODIUM: 470 mg
POTASSIUM: 370 mg
TOTAL CARBOHYDRATE: 20 g

DIETARY FIBER: 1 g
SUGARS: 1 g
PROTEIN: 30 g
PHOSPHORUS: 260 mg

SEASONED GREENS

SERVES: 8 • **SERVING SIZE:** 1/2 cup • **PREP TIME:** 10 minutes • **COOK TIME:** 30 minutes

1 large bunch of collard, mustard, or turnip greens or 1 pound frozen greens

2 fresh center-cut pork chops, fat trimmed, chopped

Hot sauce to taste

1 Rinse greens well in water. Cut into small pieces. (If using collard greens, remove tough center stem.)

2 Place greens and chopped pork in a 2-quart pan and cover with water. Season with pepper and salt, if desired. Bring to a boil and cook until tender. (Mustard or turnip greens should take about 25 minutes; collard greens take longer.)

3 When almost done, add hot sauce, if desired. Continue to cook until very tender.

CHOICES: 1 Nonstarchy Vegetable, 1 Protein, lean
CALORIES: 60

CALORIES FROM FAT: 20
TOTAL FAT: 2.0 g
SATURATED FAT: 0.7 g
TRANS FAT: 0.0 g

CHOLESTEROL: 20 mg
SODIUM: 25 mg
POTASSIUM: 150 mg
TOTAL CARBOHYDRATE: 3 g

DIETARY FIBER: 2 g
SUGARS: 0 g
PROTEIN: 8 g
PHOSPHORUS: 55 mg

CHICKEN CURRY

SERVES: 6 • **SERVING SIZE:** 3 ounces chicken + 1/3 cup curry sauce
PREP TIME: 15 minutes • **COOK TIME:** 55 minutes

2-inch piece fresh ginger root, peeled

12 cloves garlic

1 cup plus 2 tablespoons water, divided

3-pound chicken, skin removed and cut into serving-size pieces

1/2 cup fat-free plain yogurt

1 tablespoon canola oil

2 medium onions, sliced

2-inch piece cinnamon stick

6 whole cloves

3 big cardamom seeds (optional)

2 teaspoons chili powder

1 teaspoon cumin seed

1/2 teaspoon turmeric powder

2 tomatoes, peeled, seeded, and chopped

1/3 cup cilantro, chopped

1 Finely chop the ginger root and garlic and mix with 2 tablespoons water.

2 Dip the chicken in yogurt.

3 Heat a large heavy pot or Dutch oven and add oil. Sauté onion in oil until brown. Add all the spices and the yogurt-dipped chicken. Add 1/2 teaspoon salt, if desired. Continue to cook, sprinkling with additional water as required to keep from sticking.

4 Cook until chicken browns (about 10 minutes). Add 1 cup water and let simmer over low heat for about 30 minutes. Add chopped tomatoes.

5 Cook 15 more minutes or until chicken is tender. Before serving, add chopped cilantro leaves.

CHOICES: 1/2 Carbohydrate, 3 Protein, lean, 1/2 Fat
CALORIES: 210

CALORIES FROM FAT: 70
TOTAL FAT: 8.0 g
SATURATED FAT: 1.7 g
TRANS FAT: 0.0 g

CHOLESTEROL: 65 mg
SODIUM: 90 mg
POTASSIUM: 450 mg
TOTAL CARBOHYDRATE: 10 g

DIETARY FIBER: 2 g
SUGARS: 4 g
PROTEIN: 24 g
PHOSPHORUS: 210 mg

SAUCY SEAFOOD STIR-FRY

D53

SERVES: 4 • **SERVING SIZE:** 1 1/4 cups • **PREP TIME:** 10 minutes • **COOK TIME:** 10 minutes

Nonstick cooking spray
1 teaspoon canola oil
1/2 cup carrots, julienned
1 cup cauliflower florets
1 cup broccoli florets
1/4 cup red peppers, sliced
1/4 cup green peppers, sliced
1/4 cup yellow peppers, sliced
1/2 pound peeled and deveined shrimp
1/2 pound scallops
2 teaspoons tub margarine, melted
1 tablespoon reduced-fat mayonnaise
Juice of 1 lemon

1 Spray a large frying pan or wok with cooking spray. Add oil to pan and heat to medium high.

2 Stir-fry vegetables one at a time: carrots, cauliflower, then broccoli, for a total of about 4 minutes. Sprinkle with water if they start to burn. Then add peppers.

3 Add shrimp to mixture and continue cooking for about 2 minutes. Add scallops and continue cooking until shrimp turn pink and scallops turn white. Set aside.

4 In a small bowl, whip margarine and mayonnaise together until smooth. Add lemon juice.

5 Combine mayonnaise mixture with stir-fry mixture. Serve over rice.

CHOICES: 1 Nonstarchy Vegetable, 3 Protein, lean
CALORIES: 140
CALORIES FROM FAT: 40
TOTAL FAT: 4.5 g
SATURATED FAT: 0.7 g
TRANS FAT: 0.0 g
CHOLESTEROL: 85 mg
SODIUM: 390 mg
POTASSIUM: 450 mg
TOTAL CARBOHYDRATE: 8 g
DIETARY FIBER: 2 g
SUGARS: 2 g
PROTEIN: 19 g
PHOSPHORUS: 300 mg

BROCCOLI CORN CHOWDER

D54

SERVES: 10 • **SERVING SIZE:** 1 cup • **PREP TIME:** 10 minutes • **COOK TIME:** 55 minutes

2 tablespoons canola oil
1 1/2 cups fresh sliced mushrooms
1 1/2 cups chopped onion
3/4 cup flour
1/2 teaspoon white pepper
1 quart fat-free, reduced-sodium chicken broth
10 ounces frozen chopped broccoli
1 pound frozen whole-kernel corn
2 1/2 cups fat-free milk
1/4 cup pimientos, chopped

1 In a large pot, heat the oil. Add mushrooms and onion and sauté until onions are transparent.

2 Blend the flour and pepper into the mushroom mixture. Continue to cook another minute, stirring.

3 Add broth, broccoli, and corn. Bring to a boil. Reduce heat to low and simmer 15 minutes.

4 Add milk and simmer over low heat for about 30 minutes, stirring occasionally.

5 Stir in pimientos before serving.

CHOICES: 1 Starch, 1 Nonstarchy Vegetable, 1/2 Fat
CALORIES: 135
CALORIES FROM FAT: 25
TOTAL FAT: 3.0 g
SATURATED FAT: 0.3 g
TRANS FAT: 0.0 g
CHOLESTEROL: 0 mg
SODIUM: 270 mg
POTASSIUM: 400 mg
TOTAL CARBOHYDRATE: 21 g
DIETARY FIBER: 3 g
SUGARS: 6 g
PROTEIN: 7 g
PHOSPHORUS: 150 mg

BLACK BEAN CHILI

SERVES: 6 • **SERVING SIZE:** 1 1/3 cups • **PREP TIME:** 10 minutes • **COOK TIME:** 35 minutes

D55

1 large onion, chopped
1 tablespoon canola oil
1 cup water
2 tablespoons chili powder
1 teaspoon dried oregano

28-ounce can tomatoes, undrained, chopped
15-ounce can black beans, drained and rinsed
7-ounce can sweet corn, undrained

6-ounce can no-added-salt tomato paste
1 green pepper, cubed
1 red pepper, cubed
1/2 cup reduced-fat shredded Monterey Jack cheese

1 Heat oil in a large saucepan or Dutch oven until medium hot. Add onion and sauté until tender.

Add remaining ingredients except cheese.

2 Bring to a boil. Reduce heat, cover, and simmer 30

minutes or until peppers are tender, stirring occasionally.

3 Top with cheese when serving.

CHOICES: 1 Starch, 3 Nonstarchy Vegetable, 1 1/2 Fat
CALORIES: 215
CALORIES FROM FAT: 55
TOTAL FAT: 6.0 g
SATURATED FAT: 2.2 g
TRANS FAT: 0.0 g
CHOLESTEROL: 10 mg
SODIUM: 440 mg
POTASSIUM: 940 mg
TOTAL CARBOHYDRATE: 34 g
DIETARY FIBER: 9 g
SUGARS: 12 g
PROTEIN: 10 g
PHOSPHORUS: 195 mg

STUFFED VEGETARIAN PEPPERS

SERVES: 12 • **SERVING SIZE:** 1 pepper • **PREP TIME:** 35 minutes • **COOK TIME:** 1 hour

D56

2 cups uncooked couscous
4 cups boiling water
6 red peppers
6 yellow peppers

1 tablespoon plus 1/4 cup olive oil, divided
1/4 cup minced shallots
1 pound asparagus, tough ends removed

3 tablespoons tarragon
2 cups spring peas
Fresh ground pepper to taste
1/2 teaspoon paprika

1 Place couscous in a large bowl and cover with boiling water. Cover with plastic wrap and let sit for 20 minutes.

2 Preheat oven to 350°F.

3 Slice tops off peppers and remove the white membranes and seeds. Steam peppers and their tops for 5–7 minutes until tender.

4 Heat 1 tablespoon oil in a medium sauté pan and sauté the shallots until translucent. Chop the prepared asparagus into 1-inch pieces.

5 With a wooden spoon, fluff the couscous and add the shallots, asparagus tips, tarragon, peas, pepper, and 1/4 cup olive oil. Mix thoroughly.

6 Stuff the mixture into the peppers using about 2/3 cup per pepper. Cover with the tops of the peppers. Put the peppers into a large casserole dish with 1/4 inch water at the bottom. Cover and bake for 45 minutes.

7 To serve, discard each pepper top and sprinkle with paprika.

CHOICES: 1 1/2 Starch, 2 Nonstarchy Vegetable, 1 Fat
CALORIES: 215
CALORIES FROM FAT: 55
TOTAL FAT: 6.0 g
SATURATED FAT: 0.9 g
TRANS FAT: 0.0 g
CHOLESTEROL: 0 mg
SODIUM: 10 mg
POTASSIUM: 500 mg
TOTAL CARBOHYDRATE: 35 g
DIETARY FIBER: 5 g
SUGARS: 7 g
PROTEIN: 7 g
PHOSPHORUS: 100 mg

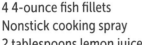
FISH CREOLE

SERVES: 4 • **SERVING SIZE:** 3 ounces fish + 1/3 cup sauce • **PREP TIME:** 15 minutes • **COOK TIME:** 25 minutes

D57

4 4-ounce fish fillets

Nonstick cooking spray

2 tablespoons lemon juice

2 tablespoons finely chopped onion

2 tablespoons tub margarine (light or low fat, 30–50% vegetable oil), divided

1/2 cup chopped green peppers

1 cup drained diced tomatoes, 1/2 cup juice reserved

Hot sauce to taste

Fresh ground pepper to taste

2 teaspoons flour

1 Preheat oven to 350°F.

2 Place fish in baking pan and lightly salt, if desired. Coat with cooking spray.

3 Mix together lemon juice, onion, and 1 tablespoon melted margarine. Pour mixture over fish. Bake uncovered or until fish flakes easily with fork (about 12–15 minutes).

4 While fish is baking, prepare creole sauce: Heat remaining 1 tablespoon margarine in medium saucepan until medium hot and then sauté green pepper. Add tomatoes, juice, hot sauce, pepper, and flour. Stir to combine. Simmer until mixture is heated.

5 To serve, place fish on plate and cover with creole sauce.

CHOICES: 1 Nonstarchy Vegetable, 3 Protein, lean
CALORIES: 175

CALORIES FROM FAT: 45
TOTAL FAT: 5.0 g
SATURATED FAT: 0.9 g
TRANS FAT: 0.0 g

CHOLESTEROL: 35 mg
SODIUM: 280 mg
POTASSIUM: 750 mg
TOTAL CARBOHYDRATE: 7 g

DIETARY FIBER: 1 g
SUGARS: 3 g
PROTEIN: 25 g
PHOSPHORUS: 280 mg

FISH IN PARCHMENT

D58

SERVES: 2 • **SERVING SIZE:** 1 pouch • **PREP TIME:** 20 minutes • **COOK TIME:** 12–15 minutes

Nonstick cooking spray

2 18-inch squares of cooking parchment

1/4 cup chopped shallots

2 4-ounce fillets of firm-fleshed fish (salmon, halibut, sole, catfish, or red snapper)

1 leek (white part), julienne cut

1 small zucchini, julienne cut

1 small carrot, julienne cut

2 medium Roma tomatoes, seeded and diced

2 tablespoons finely chopped fresh herbs (parsley, basil, or dill)

2 tablespoons fresh lemon juice

1/4 cup dry white wine

2 tablespoons flour

1 Preheat oven to 375°F. Coat both sides of parchment squares with cooking spray and fold each in half. Open halves back up.

2 Place chopped shallots in the middle of one half of each piece of parchment.

3 Top shallots with fish. Lightly season fish with pepper and salt, if desired.

4 On top of fish, place leek, zucchini, carrot, and tomatoes. Sprinkle with herbs.

5 Sprinkle lemon juice and wine on top of fish and vegetables.

6 Combine flour with enough water to moisten. To seal packages, brush the edges of the parchment with the flour-water mixture. Bring edges of parchment together and press down to seal.

7 Place on a baking sheet and bake about 12–15 minutes.

8 To serve, place pouch on plate and cut an "X" in the top. Peel back four corners.

CHOICES: 3 Nonstarchy Vegetable, 3 Protein, lean
CALORIES: 240

CALORIES FROM FAT: 65
TOTAL FAT: 7.0 g
SATURATED FAT: 1.5 g
TRANS FAT: 0.0 g

CHOLESTEROL: 50 mg
SODIUM: 85 mg
POTASSIUM: 940 mg
TOTAL CARBOHYDRATE: 16 g

DIETARY FIBER: 3 g
SUGARS: 5 g
PROTEIN: 27 g
PHOSPHORUS: 340 mg

PRUNE-STUFFED TENDERLOIN

SERVES: 4 • **SERVING SIZE:** 2 1/2-inch slice • **PREP TIME:** 30 minutes • **COOK TIME:** 50 minutes

15 dried pitted prunes, coarsely chopped

1/3 cup fat-free, reduced-sodium chicken broth

1 teaspoon canola oil

1/4 cup chopped celery

1/4 cup chopped onion

3 slices multigrain bread, slightly dry and cubed

1/8 teaspoon poultry seasoning

1 pound pork tenderloin

1 clove garlic, crushed

1/8 teaspoon fennel seeds

Nonstick cooking spray

1 tablespoon tub margarine (60–70% vegetable oil, no trans fat), melted

1 Bring prunes and broth to a boil in a saucepan. Remove from heat and let stand for 10 minutes.

2 Heat oil in a small sauté pan and cook celery and onion until tender. Preheat oven to 500°F.

3 Place bread cubes and poultry seasoning in a large bowl. Toss to mix. Add celery, onions, prunes, and broth. Toss lightly to blend. Add more broth if dressing is too dry.

4 Trim excess fat from tenderloin. Cut lengthwise to within 1/2 inch of each end and almost to the bottom, leaving bottom connected. Open the meat and pound sides of pocket to about 1/4 inch thickness. Combine garlic, fennel seeds, and pepper and salt, if desired, and rub on the inside of pocket. Spoon stuffing into opening of tenderloin. Press gently to close. Tie tenderloin securely with heavy string at 1-inch intervals.

5 Place tenderloin on roasting rack coated with cooking spray. Place rack in roasting pan. Place tenderloin in oven. Immediately reduce temperature to 350°F. Cook 20 minutes, then brush on melted margarine and cook an additional 10–15 minutes or until inserted instant-read thermometer reaches 155°F.

6 Remove from oven, cover with foil, and let stand 10 minutes before slicing into 4 equal servings.

CHOICES: 1 Starch, 1 Fruit, 3 Protein, lean	**CALORIES FROM FAT:** 65	**CHOLESTEROL:** 60 mg	**DIETARY FIBER:** 4 g
	TOTAL FAT: 7.0 g	**SODIUM:** 195 mg	**SUGARS:** 14 g
	SATURATED FAT: 1.7 g	**POTASSIUM:** 680 mg	**PROTEIN:** 26 g
CALORIES: 280	**TRANS FAT:** 0.0 g	**TOTAL CARBOHYDRATE:** 30 g	**PHOSPHORUS:** 270 mg

ORIENTAL CHICKEN

SERVES: 4 • **SERVING SIZE:** 1 chicken thigh + 1 cup vegetables with sauce
PREP TIME: 10 minutes • **COOK TIME:** 30 minutes

1 tablespoon canola oil

4 chicken thighs, skin and fat removed

1/2 cup dry white wine

1/4 cup chopped onions or scallions

1/2 cup sliced celery

1 teaspoon minced fresh ginger

8 ounces fresh mushrooms, washed and sliced

4 ounces (1/2 8-ounce can) water chestnuts, drained

2 tablespoons light soy sauce

1 teaspoon brown sugar

1/4 teaspoon garlic powder

1/4 teaspoon dried red pepper flakes

8 ounce snow peas, fresh or frozen

1 Place canola oil in a heavy saucepan and heat until medium hot.

2 Sauté chicken in saucepan until seared on both sides. Remove from pan and set aside.

3 With heat still on, add wine to empty pan to deglaze, scraping up bits of residue of the seared chicken. Cook until wine is reduced by half.

4 Meanwhile, add onions, celery, and ginger to pan and sauté until onions and celery are translucent.

5 Add mushrooms and water chestnuts to pan and continue cooking another 2–3 minutes.

6 Add soy sauce, brown sugar, garlic powder, and red pepper to pan and stir well.

7 Return chicken to pan with other ingredients. Cover and cook for 15 minutes, or until chicken is almost done.

8 Add snow peas to mixture and cook an additional 5 minutes or until snow peas are tender.

CHOICES: 2 Nonstarchy Vegetable, 2 Protein, lean, 1 Fat
CALORIES: 210
CALORIES FROM FAT: 80
TOTAL FAT: 9.0 g
SATURATED FAT: 1.9 g
TRANS FAT: 0.0 g
CHOLESTEROL: 50 mg
SODIUM: 355 mg
POTASSIUM: 600 mg
TOTAL CARBOHYDRATE: 11 g
DIETARY FIBER: 3 g
SUGARS: 6 g
PROTEIN: 18 g
PHOSPHORUS: 245 mg

SEAFOOD GUMBO

 D61

SERVES: 8 • **SERVING SIZE:** 1 cup • **PREP TIME:** 10 minutes • **COOK TIME:** 20 minutes

2 teaspoons canola oil
2 medium onions, chopped
1 cup chopped celery
1 clove garlic, minced
1/2 large green pepper, chopped
1 tablespoon chopped parsley

1 teaspoon ground thyme
1 cup canned tomatoes, with juice
2 cups low-fat, low-sodium
  chicken broth
1/4 cup tomato paste
1 pound small or medium shrimp,

peeled and deveined
1 pound orange roughy or other
  firm, boneless fish, cut into
  bite-size pieces
2 cups sliced fresh or frozen okra

1 Heat oil in a heavy large Dutch oven with cover.

2 Sauté onions, celery, and garlic until onion is translucent.

3 Add green pepper, parsley, thyme, canned tomatoes, and chicken broth. Bring to a boil. Reduce heat and cook about 3–4 minutes, or until stock is reduced a bit.

4 Add tomato paste, stirring until incorporated.

5 Add shrimp, fish, and okra, gently stirring. Cover and continue simmering until shrimp and fish are done.

CHOICES: 2 Nonstarchy Vegetable, 2 Protein, lean
CALORIES: 140
CALORIES FROM FAT: 20
TOTAL FAT: 2.0 g
SATURATED FAT: 0.3 g
TRANS FAT: 0.0 g
CHOLESTEROL: 100 mg
SODIUM: 250 mg
POTASSIUM: 550 mg
TOTAL CARBOHYDRATE: 10 g
DIETARY FIBER: 3 g
SUGARS: 5 g
PROTEIN: 20 g
PHOSPHORUS: 210 mg

BARBECUED CHICKEN

D62

SERVES: 2 • **SERVING SIZE:** 1 thigh + 1 drumstick
PREP TIME: 10 minutes + 2 hours marinate time • **COOK TIME:** 10 minutes

2 chicken thighs and 2
  drumsticks, skinless and
  boneless
1/2 cup *Barbecue Sauce*,
  divided (page 169)

1 Marinate raw chicken pieces in 1/4 cup barbecue sauce in a resealable plastic bag for at least 2 hours in the refrigerator. Be sure that the chicken is entirely covered with the sauce.

2 Grill the chicken over medium coals, and brush it with the remaining 1/4 cup barbecue sauce during the last 2 minutes of cooking. Thighs will need about 5 minutes of cooking; check for doneness by making sure it is not pink inside.

CHOICES: 4 Protein, lean
CALORIES: 200
CALORIES FROM FAT: 70
TOTAL FAT: 8.0 g
SATURATED FAT: 2.3 g
TRANS FAT: 0.0 g
CHOLESTEROL: 90 mg
SODIUM: 260 mg
POTASSIUM: 410 mg
TOTAL CARBOHYDRATE: 3 g
DIETARY FIBER: 1 g
SUGARS: 2 g
PROTEIN: 26 g
PHOSPHORUS: 235 mg

PORK BOK CHOY SAUTÉ

SERVES: 2 • **SERVING SIZE:** 3 ounces pork + 1 cup vegetables • **PREP TIME:** 10 minutes • **COOK TIME:** 10 minutes

1 tablespoon sesame oil

1 clove garlic, crushed

8-ounce pork tenderloin, thinly sliced

1 cup sliced shiitake or other mushrooms

1 1/2 cups sliced bok choy, with leaves

4 ounces (1/2 8-ounce can) water chestnuts, drained

1 tablespoon light soy sauce

1 Add oil to a large skillet or wok over medium-high heat and cook garlic 1 minute.

2 Add pork, stirring constantly, and cook 3–5 minutes. Add mushrooms. Cook, stirring constantly, for 1 minute.

3 Add bok choy and water chestnuts. Cook, stirring constantly, for 2–3 minutes.

4 Add soy sauce; toss to coat.

CHOICES: 2 Nonstarchy Vegetable, 3 Protein, lean, 1 Fat
CALORIES: 225
CALORIES FROM FAT: 90
TOTAL FAT: 10.0 g
SATURATED FAT: 2.0 g
TRANS FAT: 0.0 g
CHOLESTEROL: 60 mg
SODIUM: 345 mg
POTASSIUM: 680 mg
TOTAL CARBOHYDRATE: 9 g
DIETARY FIBER: 3 g
SUGARS: 3 g
PROTEIN: 25 g
PHOSPHORUS: 265 mg

BLACK BEAN CAKES

SERVES: 2 • **SERVING SIZE:** 2 cakes • **PREP TIME:** 10 minutes • **COOK TIME:** 10 minutes

1 1/4 cups cooked black beans, slightly mashed

1/2 cup chopped onion

1/2 cup chopped cilantro or fresh parsley

2 tablespoons Asian chili-garlic paste or plain tomato paste

1/4 cup egg substitute

2 tablespoons fat-free or low-fat (1%) milk

1/4 cup dry bread crumbs

2 tablespoons olive oil

1 In a medium-large bowl, thoroughly mix all ingredients except bread crumbs and olive oil. Add salt and pepper, if desired.

2 Add bread crumbs to mixture and form into 4 patties. Heat a sauté pan with oil and gently slide patties into pan. Sauté until brown and crisp on both sides.

CHOICES: 2 1/2 Starch, 2 Protein, lean, 2 Fat
CALORIES: 365
CALORIES FROM FAT: 135
TOTAL FAT: 15.0 g
SATURATED FAT: 2.2 g
TRANS FAT: 0.0 g
CHOLESTEROL: 0 mg
SODIUM: 290 mg
POTASSIUM: 710 mg
TOTAL CARBOHYDRATE: 43 g
DIETARY FIBER: 11 g
SUGARS: 8 g
PROTEIN: 16 g
PHOSPHORUS: 220 mg

HAWAIIAN KABOBS

SERVES: 4 • **SERVING SIZE:** 2 kabobs • **PREP TIME:** 15 minutes + 1 hour marinate time • **COOK TIME:** 30 minutes

1 tablespoon light soy sauce
1/4 cup pineapple juice
1/2 teaspoon garlic powder
1 teaspoon ground ginger
1/2 teaspoon dry mustard
1/4 teaspoon pepper

2 tablespoons canola oil
14 ounces boneless, skinless chicken breasts, cut into 1-inch cubes
2 cups fresh or juice-packed pineapple chunks

2 medium green peppers, cut in chunks
16 medium mushrooms
8 cherry tomatoes

1 Combine first seven ingredients in a small saucepan and bring to a boil. Reduce heat and simmer 5 minutes. Let cool.

2 Pour mixture into a shallow dish and add chicken, tossing gently to coat. Cover and marinate at least 1 hour in the refrigerator, stirring mixture occasionally.

3 Remove chicken from marinade, reserving marinade. Alternate chicken, pineapple, green pepper, mushrooms, and tomatoes on eight skewers.

4 Grill over hot coals 20 minutes or until done, turning and basting frequently with marinade.

CHOICES: 1 Fruit, 1 Nonstarchy Vegetable, 3 Protein, lean, 1 Fat
CALORIES: 265

CALORIES FROM FAT: 90
TOTAL FAT: 10.0 g
SATURATED FAT: 1.3 g
TRANS FAT: 0.0 g

CHOLESTEROL: 60 mg
SODIUM: 200 mg
POTASSIUM: 710 mg
TOTAL CARBOHYDRATE: 20 g

DIETARY FIBER: 4 g
SUGARS: 13 g
PROTEIN: 25 g
PHOSPHORUS: 255 mg

CACTUS (NOPALES) SALAD

SERVES: 7 • **SERVING SIZE:** 1/2 cup • **PREP TIME:** 15 minutes • **COOK TIME:** 5 minutes + 1 hour cool time

1 pound fresh or canned nopales
1/2 large white onion, cut into chunks
1/2 teaspoon salt
2 medium tomatoes, peeled and chopped, or a 14-ounce can diced tomatoes, drained
1/2 cup finely chopped cilantro
2 teaspoons fresh lime juice
1/2 medium avocado, cubed
1/4 cup shredded Mexican cheese

1 Rinse fresh nopales and pat dry. Cut into 1/2-inch pieces. (Some people prefer to peel them with a vegetable peeler, while others simply remove the thorns and the least tender part, close to where the leaf was cut from the plant.)

2 Cook in boiling water with onion and salt for 5 minutes. Or drain canned nopales and cut into pieces.

3 In a medium bowl, combine nopales, tomato, cilantro, and lime juice. Refrigerate at least 1 hour. Before serving, add avocado and garnish with cheese. Serve with tortillas.

CHOICES: 1 Nonstarchy Vegetable, 1/2 Fat
CALORIES: 55

CALORIES FROM FAT: 25
TOTAL FAT: 3.0 g
SATURATED FAT: 1.1 g
TRANS FAT: 0.0 g

CHOLESTEROL: 5 mg
SODIUM: 210 mg
POTASSIUM: 310 mg
TOTAL CARBOHYDRATE: 6 g

DIETARY FIBER: 3 g
SUGARS: 3 g
PROTEIN: 2 g
PHOSPHORUS: 50 mg

BEEF STEW

SERVES: 5 • **SERVING SIZE:** 1 cup • **PREP TIME:** 5 minutes • **COOK TIME:** 3 hours 10 minutes

D67

1 tablespoon olive or canola oil

1 1/2 pounds flank steak, cut into bite-sized pieces

1 medium onion, peeled and chopped

2 cloves garlic, minced

1/2 medium green bell pepper, chopped

1/2 medium red bell pepper, chopped

4 cups low-fat, low-sodium beef stock

1 carrot, cut into 1-inch pieces

2 celery stalks, trimmed, cut into 1-inch pieces

1 Anaheim pepper, roasted and chopped

2–3 jalapeño, serrano, Thai, or yellow peppers, chopped, to taste

15-ounce can crushed tomatoes with juice

2 whole cloves

4–5 black peppercorns

1/2 teaspoon thyme

1/2 teaspoon cumin

1/2 teaspoon black pepper

1 Heat the oil over medium-high heat in a large stockpot and sauté the meat, onion, garlic, and bell peppers until meat is browned, about 8–10 minutes. Stir frequently.

2 Add remaining ingredients and bring to a boil. Cover, reduce heat, and simmer 2–3 hours. Remove whole cloves and peppercorns before serving.

CHOICES: 3 Nonstarchy Vegetable, 4 Protein, lean, 1/2 Fat	**CALORIES FROM FAT:** 90	**CHOLESTEROL:** 45 mg	**DIETARY FIBER:** 4 g
	TOTAL FAT: 10.0 g	**SODIUM:** 295 mg	**SUGARS:** 9 g
	SATURATED FAT: 3.4 g	**POTASSIUM:** 980 mg	**PROTEIN:** 32 g
CALORIES: 285	**TRANS FAT:** 0.0 g	**TOTAL CARBOHYDRATE:** 17 g	**PHOSPHORUS:** 300 mg

TOWNSON'S TORTILLA SOUP

D68

SERVES: 4 • **SERVING SIZE:** 1 1/3 cups soup + 1 1/2 tortilla crisps + 1 tablespoon cheese
PREP TIME: 10 minutes • **COOK TIME:** 35 minutes

6 6-inch corn tortillas

Nonstick cooking spray

1 tablespoon canola oil

1 medium onion, peeled and finely chopped

1 clove garlic, minced

14.5-ounce can diced tomatoes with juice

2 tablespoons chopped cilantro

4 cups low-fat, low-sodium chicken broth

1 fresh epazote leaf (Mexican tea), if available, or 1/4 teaspoon dried epazote

1/4 teaspoon chili powder

1/4 cup shredded reduced-fat jack or muenster cheese

1 Heat oven to 400°F. Cut tortillas into thin strips. Place on baking sheet that has been coated with nonstick cooking spray. Bake until crisp, about 8–10 minutes.

2 Heat oil in small skillet and sauté onion and garlic for 4–5 minutes.

3 In a blender or food processor, pureé tomatoes, onion, garlic, and cilantro.

4 In a large stockpot, bring tomato mixture and broth to boil. Cover, reduce heat, and simmer 15–20 minutes. Stir once or twice.

5 Add epazote and cook for 5 minutes.

6 Stir in chili powder before serving. Add tortilla strips now or as soup is eaten. Garnish each serving with 1 tablespoon cheese.

CHOICES: 1 Starch, 2 Nonstarchy Vegetable, 1 Fat	**CALORIES FROM FAT:** 55	**CHOLESTEROL:** 10 mg	**DIETARY FIBER:** 4 g
	TOTAL FAT: 6.0 g	**SODIUM:** 310 mg	**SUGARS:** 5 g
	SATURATED FAT: 1.5 g	**POTASSIUM:** 530 mg	**PROTEIN:** 8 g
CALORIES: 180	**TRANS FAT:** 0.0 g	**TOTAL CARBOHYDRATE:** 25 g	**PHOSPHORUS:** 260 mg

MEAT AND VEGETABLE EMPANADAS

SERVES: 12 • **SERVING SIZE:** 1 empanada • **PREP TIME:** 15 minutes • **COOK TIME:** 40 minutes

1 tablespoon canola oil

1/2 onion, chopped fine

1 cup finely diced carrots

1/2 cup finely shredded cabbage

1/2 green or red bell pepper, chopped fine

1 tablespoon thinly sliced green olives

1 clove garlic, crushed

1 tablespoon chopped fresh parsley or 1 teaspoon dried parsley

1/2 tablespoon chopped fresh basil or 1/2 teaspoon dried basil

1/2 teaspoon salt

1/4 teaspoon black pepper

1 pound 96% lean ground beef

1 teaspoon cornstarch

1/2 cup low-fat, reduced-sodium beef broth

1 hard-boiled egg, chopped

1 recipe *Low-Fat Empanada Dough* (page 137)

1 Heat oil in nonstick skillet over medium-high heat. Sauté all ingredients—except the meat, cornstarch, broth, egg, and dough—for 10 minutes.

2 Add the meat and cook for 15 minutes, stirring frequently. Dissolve the cornstarch in the broth. Add to skillet and reduce heat to low. Cook until almost all of the liquid has evaporated. Refrigerate filling overnight.

3 Heat the oven to 400°F. Place 2 tablespoons filling in center of each dough circle. Put a little egg in each turnover. Moisten edges with water and seal with a fork.

4 Bake on a baking sheet that has been coated with nonstick cooking spray for 15 minutes or until golden brown.

CHOICES: 1 Starch, 1 Protein, lean, 1 1/2 Fat
CALORIES: 195

CALORIES FROM FAT: 80
TOTAL FAT: 9.0 g
SATURATED FAT: 2.2 g
TRANS FAT: 0.1 g

CHOLESTEROL: 49 mg
SODIUM: 310 mg
POTASSIUM: 260 mg
TOTAL CARBOHYDRATE: 19 g

DIETARY FIBER: 2 g
SUGARS: 1 g
PROTEIN: 11 g
PHOSPHORUS: 135 mg

LOW-FAT EMPANADA DOUGH

SERVES: 12 • **SERVING SIZE:** 1 empanada • **PREP TIME:** 25 minutes • **CHILL TIME:** 8 hours

1 cup all-purpose flour

1 cup masa harina (corn flour)

1/2 teaspoon salt

6 tablespoons tub margarine (60–70% vegetable oil, no trans fat), cut into 6 pieces

1/2 cup ice water or as needed

1 egg, beaten

2 teaspoons water

1 In the bowl of a food processor, using the metal blade, blend flour, masa harina, and salt. Add margarine and process 5–10 seconds until mixture has the consistency of coarse meal.

2 With processor running, add 1/2 cup ice water. Stop processor as soon as dough begins to form a ball. Add more water by the tablespoon, if needed.

3 Remove from bowl; form a pliable ball. Use the dough immediately or wrap in plastic and refrigerate for several hours or overnight.

4 Heat oven to 400°F. Remove dough from refrigerator and divide in half, keeping remaining half covered. Roll each half into a log about 1 1/2 inches in diameter. Cut each log into 6 equal pieces. Roll out each piece on lightly floured surface into a circle about 5 inches in diameter.

5 Spoon 2 tablespoons filling onto the center of the circle. Moisten the edges of the dough with water and bring them together, forming the turnover. Seal edges with the tines of a fork.

6 Place empanadas on a cookie sheet that has been sprayed with nonstick cooking spray or covered with parchment paper. Combine a beaten egg with 2 teaspoons water to create an egg wash. Brush tops with egg wash and bake according to filling instructions.

CHOICES: 1 Starch, 1 Fat
CALORIES: 115

CALORIES FROM FAT: 45
TOTAL FAT: 5.0 g
SATURATED FAT: 1.0 g
TRANS FAT: 0.0 g

CHOLESTEROL: 10 mg
SODIUM: 145 mg
POTASSIUM: 45 mg
TOTAL CARBOHYDRATE: 16 g

DIETARY FIBER: 1 g
SUGARS: 0 g
PROTEIN: 2 g
PHOSPHORUS: 40 mg

CHILEAN CORN PIE

SERVES: 6 • **SERVING SIZE:** 1 slice • **PREP TIME:** 30 minutes • **COOK TIME:** 1 hour 20 minutes

MEAT FILLING

1 tablespoon canola oil

3 medium onions, peeled and finely chopped

2–3 cloves garlic, minced

1/8–1/4 teaspoon *Habañero Paste* (page 170)

1/2 teaspoon salt

1/2 teaspoon paprika

1/2 teaspoon cumin

Ground black pepper, to taste

1 pound 96% lean ground beef or finely diced boneless, skinless chicken breast

1/4 cup low-fat, low-sodium beef or chicken broth, homemade or canned

CORN DOUGH

6 ears fresh corn or 3 cups frozen corn, thawed

2 tablespoons olive oil

1/4 teaspoon salt

1 tablespoon fat-free milk (optional)

2 hard-boiled eggs, sliced into six slices

1 Prepare the meat filling: Heat oil in a medium skillet over medium heat. Sauté onion and garlic for 2 minutes. Stir in seasonings and 2 tablespoons raisins, if desired. Add meat and cook for 4–5 minutes. Drain fat, then add broth. Cover, reduce heat, and simmer 10–15 minutes. You can cook this filling in advance and refrigerate it.

2 Prepare the corn dough: Cut corn kernels from cobs and finely chop the kernels. Grate cobs to capture remaining kernels; then add 1/8 teaspoon basil, if desired. Heat oil in medium skillet over low heat. Add corn and salt, and cook until corn bubbles and thickens, about 10–15 minutes. If dough is too runny, add 1 tablespoon masa harina. If corn dough is too thick, add milk.

3 Prepare the pie: Heat oven to 375°F. Spray a loaf pan with nonstick cooking spray. Spread half the corn dough in the bottom of the pan, spread the filling on top, then cover with remaining corn dough. Top with egg slices and sprinkle with 1 tablespoon sugar, if desired. Bake until sugar melts and forms a golden crust on the pie, 30–45 minutes. If you are not using sugar, bake until pie is golden brown.

CHOICES: 1 Starch, 1 Nonstarchy Vegetable, 2 Protein, lean, 1 1/2 Fat
CALORIES: 270

CALORIES FROM FAT: 108
TOTAL FAT: 12.0 g
SATURATED FAT: 2.9 g
TRANS FAT: 0.2 g

CHOLESTEROL: 105 mg
SODIUM: 385 mg
POTASSIUM: 570 mg
TOTAL CARBOHYDRATE: 21 g

DIETARY FIBER: 3 g
SUGARS: 5 g
PROTEIN: 22 g
PHOSPHORUS: 265 mg

CHICKEN BREAST WITH CHIPOTLES

SERVES: 4 • **SERVING SIZE:** 3 ounces chicken + 1 1/2 tablespoons mushrooms + 1/3 cup sauce
PREP TIME: 10 minutes + 1 hour chill time • **COOK TIME:** 40 minutes

1 tablespoon prepared mustard
1/4 teaspoon salt
1/4 teaspoon black pepper
1 tablespoon olive oil, divided use

4 (4-ounce) boneless, skinless chicken breast halves
1 cup sliced mushrooms
1/2 cup fat-free half-and-half

3/4 cup low-fat, low-sodium chicken broth
2–3 chopped, seeded chipotle chilies or to taste
2 cloves garlic, minced

1 Mix mustard, salt, and pepper and spread over chicken breasts. Refrigerate chicken for at least 1 hour.

2 Heat 1/2 tablespoon oil in a large skillet over medium-high heat and sauté mushrooms for 4–5 minutes, stirring constantly. Remove mushrooms from skillet and keep warm. Heat remaining 1/2 tablespoon oil, add chicken, and brown for 15–20 minutes, turning once.

3 Meanwhile, combine half-and-half and broth in a small saucepan over medium-low heat. Add chilies and garlic and bring to a simmer. Cook for 10 minutes or until mixture thickens slightly, stirring constantly. Place mixture in blender and blend until smooth.

4 Place chicken on a serving platter, pour sauce over chicken, top with mushrooms, and serve.

CHOICES: 4 Protein, lean
CALORIES: 190
CALORIES FROM FAT: 65
TOTAL FAT: 7.0 g

SATURATED FAT: 1.6 g
TRANS FAT: 0.0 g
CHOLESTEROL: 70 mg
SODIUM: 295 mg

POTASSIUM: 440 mg
TOTAL CARBOHYDRATE: 5 g
DIETARY FIBER: 1 g
SUGARS: 2 g

PROTEIN: 26 g
PHOSPHORUS: 265 mg

MEAT KABOB MEDLEY

SERVES: 6 • **SERVING SIZE:** 2 kabobs • **PREP TIME:** 10 minutes • **COOK TIME:** 10–15 minutes

1/2 pound beef top sirloin, cut into 12 pieces
1/2 pound boneless pork loin, cut into 12 pieces
1/2 pound boneless, skinless chicken breast, cut into 12 pieces

1 medium green bell pepper, cut into 12 chunks
1 medium red bell pepper, cut into 12 chunks
2 medium onions, each cut into 12 chunks

1 Place 1 piece of beef, pork, and chicken on each of 12 skewers, alternating with chunks of pepper and onion.

2 Grill or broil about 6 inches from the heat source for 10–15 minutes, turning kabobs frequently.

CHOICES: 1 Nonstarchy Vegetable, 3 Protein, lean
CALORIES: 170

CALORIES FROM FAT: 30
TOTAL FAT: 5 g
SATURATED FAT: 1.7 g
TRANS FAT: 0.0 g

CHOLESTEROL: 55 mg
SODIUM: 50 mg
POTASSIUM: 430 mg
TOTAL CARBOHYDRATE: 7 g

DIETARY FIBER: 2 g
SUGARS: 4 g
PROTEIN: 24 g
PHOSPHORUS: 200 mg

MEATBALLS PUEBLA STYLE

SERVES: 4 • **SERVING SIZE:** 3 meatballs • **PREP TIME:** 30 minutes • **COOK TIME:** 55 minutes

MEATBALLS
1 pound 96% lean ground beef
1/2 cup cooked rice
1 small onion, finely chopped
2 cloves garlic, minced
1 egg, lightly beaten
1/4 cup bread crumbs
1/4 teaspoon black pepper

1/4 teaspoon dried mint or 1 teaspoon chopped fresh mint
1 tablespoon chopped fresh cilantro, leaves only
1/2 cup no-added-salt, fat-free beef broth

SAUCE
1 1/2 cups no-added-salt tomato sauce

1 1/2 cups water
1–2 chipotle chilies, put through the blender with 2 tablespoons water
1 teaspoon cinnamon
1 teaspoon cumin
1/8 teaspoon cloves
1/4 teaspoon black pepper

1 Heat oven to 350°F. In a large bowl, combine all meatball ingredients except beef broth and mix well. Shape into 12 meatballs. Place meatballs in baking dish and bake for 15 minutes.

2 Combine all sauce ingredients in a medium saucepan and bring to a boil. Lower heat and simmer for 15 minutes.

3 Pour beef broth over meatballs and turn. Bake 10 more minutes. Remove meatballs from oven and drain on paper towels.

4 Add meatballs to simmering chipotle sauce, cover, and cook 15 more minutes.

CHOICES: 1/2 Starch, 2 Nonstarchy Vegetable, 3 Protein, lean, 1/2 Fat
CALORIES: 255
CALORIES FROM FAT: 65
TOTAL FAT: 7.0 g
SATURATED FAT: 2.5 g
TRANS FAT: 0.3 g
CHOLESTEROL: 115 mg
SODIUM: 290 mg
POTASSIUM: 840 mg
TOTAL CARBOHYDRATE: 21 g
DIETARY FIBER: 3 g
SUGARS: 6 g
PROTEIN: 29 g
PHOSPHORUS: 320 mg

COLD PEANUT NOODLES

D75

SERVES: 8 • **SERVING SIZE:** 1 cup • **PREP TIME:** 10 minutes • **COOK TIME:** 10 minutes + 8 hours chill time

1 pound whole-wheat spaghetti
2 tablespoons sesame oil
1 tablespoon fresh minced ginger
1 tablespoon chopped garlic

1/4 cup no-added-salt peanut butter
2 tablespoons lite soy sauce
2 tablespoons rice vinegar
1 tablespoon lemon juice

3/4 cup chopped green onion
1 cup chopped, seeded cucumber
1 tablespoon chopped unsalted peanuts

1 Cook spaghetti according to package directions and drain. Whisk together remaining ingredients except onion, cucumber, and peanuts. Mix dressing with cooked pasta.

2 Add onion and cucumber and mix gently. Chill in refrigerator, covered, for several hours before serving. Sprinkle chopped peanuts over top of each serving.

CHOICES: 3 Starch, 1 Protein, lean, 1 Fat
CALORIES: 290
CALORIES FROM FAT: 80
TOTAL FAT: 9.0 g
SATURATED FAT: 1.5 g
TRANS FAT: 0.0 g
CHOLESTEROL: 0 mg
SODIUM: 145 mg
POTASSIUM: 180 mg
TOTAL CARBOHYDRATE: 45 g
DIETARY FIBER: 8 g
SUGARS: 1 g
PROTEIN: 11 g
PHOSPHORUS: 155 mg

DINNER

CHICKEN FAJITAS

D76

SERVES: 4 • **SERVING SIZE:** 1/2 cup + 1 tortilla
PREP TIME: 10 minutes + 2 hours marinate time • **COOK TIME:** 10 minutes

1 clove garlic, minced
2 1/2 teaspoons canola oil
2 1/2 teaspoons lemon juice
1 1/2 tablespoons light soy sauce
Fresh ground pepper
2 teaspoons salt-free Mexican (or pizza) seasoning
1 pound boneless, skinless chicken breasts
2 teaspoons canola oil
2/3 medium onion, thinly sliced
1 medium green pepper, thinly sliced
Nonstick cooking spray
4 6-inch whole-wheat flour tortillas

1 Make marinade by combining garlic, oil, lemon juice, soy sauce, pepper, and seasoning.

2 Cut chicken into thin strips. Add chicken to marinade, toss to coat evenly, and marinate in refrigerator for up to 2 hours. Stir mixture occasionally to recoat meat.

3 In a nonstick skillet, heat a small amount of oil on medium-high heat. Add sliced onions and peppers.

Sauté, stirring occasionally, until onion is slightly brown, but still crisp and tender.

4 In another skillet sprayed with nonstick cooking spray, sauté chicken with only a small amount of oil over medium heat until meat is no longer pink. Serve with onions and peppers on tortilla.

CHOICES: 1 Starch, 1 Nonstarchy Vegetable, 3 Protein, lean, 1 Fat
CALORIES: 280
CALORIES FROM FAT: 100
TOTAL FAT: 11.0 g
SATURATED FAT: 2.5 g
TRANS FAT: 0.0 g
CHOLESTEROL: 65 mg
SODIUM: 400 mg
POTASSIUM: 400 mg
TOTAL CARBOHYDRATE: 18 g
DIETARY FIBER: 4 g
SUGARS: 3 g
PROTEIN: 28 g
PHOSPHORUS: 295 mg

ORANGE ROUGHY PICANTE

D77

SERVES: 4 • **SERVING SIZE:** 4 ounce • **PREP TIME:** 10 minutes • **COOK TIME:** 5 minutes

1 orange roughy fillet, about 1 pound
1/2 16-ounce jar mild salsa
1/4 cup chopped onion
1/4 cup chopped green pepper
1/4 cup sliced fresh mushrooms
1/4 cup grated cheddar cheese

1 Place fish in microwave-safe dish. Cover with salsa. Sprinkle with onion, green pepper, and mushrooms.

2 Place a lid over dish and vent. Microwave on high for 2 minutes. Stop microwave, uncover, and place grated cheese on top of fish. Cover again and

continue cooking for 2 additional minutes or until fish flakes easily with fork.

3 Divide fish into 4 equal portions. Serve with rice and green beans.

Note: To prepare in conventional oven, bake at 400°F for 15 minutes.

CHOICES: 1 Nonstarchy Vegetable, 3 Protein, lean
CALORIES: 140
CALORIES FROM FAT: 30
TOTAL FAT: 3.5 g
SATURATED FAT: 1.6 g
TRANS FAT: 0.1 g
CHOLESTEROL: 80 mg
SODIUM: 430 mg
POTASSIUM: 380 mg
TOTAL CARBOHYDRATE: 5 g
DIETARY FIBER: 1 g
SUGARS: 3 g
PROTEIN: 23 g
PHOSPHORUS: 150 mg

SUMMER MAIN DISH SALAD

SERVES: 4 • **SERVING SIZE:** 3 ounces meat + 1 1/2 tablespoons dressing + 1 1/3 cups vegetables + 1 cup greens
PREP TIME: 10 minutes • **COOK TIME:** 10 minutes

1 cup frozen corn kernels
4 teaspoons canola oil
3 cloves garlic, sliced
1/4 cup wine vinegar
1 tablespoon Dijon mustard
Fresh ground pepper to taste
1/4 teaspoon sugar
12 ounces grilled sirloin, sliced
1 cup cubed cooked potatoes
1 cup sliced green onions
1/2 cup thinly sliced carrots
1 cup diced red pepper
1 cup diced green pepper
4 cups salad greens

1 Cook corn according to package directions.

2 In a small saucepan, heat oil; sauté garlic until golden brown.

3 Remove from heat and cool; strain and reserve oil; discard garlic.

4 In a large bowl, combine reserved oil, vinegar, mustard, pepper, and sugar. Add 1/2 teaspoon salt, if desired.

5 Combine oil mixture with corn, sirloin, potatoes, green onions, carrots, and both kinds of peppers. Mix well, cover, and chill.

6 Serve in a bowl lined with salad greens.

CHOICES: 1 Starch, 2 Nonstarchy Vegetable, 3 Protein, lean, 1 Fat
CALORIES: 310
CALORIES FROM FAT: 90
TOTAL FAT: 10.0 g
SATURATED FAT: 2.3 g
TRANS FAT: 0.2 g
CHOLESTEROL: 50 mg
SODIUM: 175 mg
POTASSIUM: 960 mg
TOTAL CARBOHYDRATE: 26 g
DIETARY FIBER: 5 g
SUGARS: 7 g
PROTEIN: 30 g
PHOSPHORUS: 305 mg

PORCUPINE MEATBALLS

SERVES: 2 • **SERVING SIZE:** 3 meatballs • **PREP TIME:** 10 minutes • **COOK TIME:** 25 minutes

8 ounces 96% lean ground beef
2/3 cup cooked brown rice
1 1/2 tablespoons dried minced onion
1/4 teaspoon pepper
1/8 teaspoon dried oregano
1 cup no-added-salt tomato sauce
1 cup water

1 Mix beef, rice, onion, and seasonings until well blended. Form into six meatballs.

2 Heat a medium sauté pan until medium hot. Place meatballs in hot pan; turn when slightly browned. Continue to sear on all sides just until browned but not fully cooked.

3 Drain pan of excess grease and pour tomato sauce and water on top of meatballs. Cover and simmer until meatballs are done, about 15–20 minutes.

CHOICES: 1 Starch, 2 Nonstarchy Vegetable, 3 Protein, lean
CALORIES: 270
CALORIES FROM FAT: 60
TOTAL FAT: 7.0 g
SATURATED FAT: 2.9 g
TRANS FAT: 0.1 g
CHOLESTEROL: 70 mg
SODIUM: 85 mg
POTASSIUM: 850 mg
TOTAL CARBOHYDRATE: 27 g
DIETARY FIBER: 3 g
SUGARS: 6 g
PROTEIN: 26 g
POTASSIUM: 315 mg

RECIPE PHOTO ON PREVIOUS PAGE:

Shrimp and Pea Salad, pg. L39

DILLED POTATO SALAD

SERVES: 4 • **SERVING SIZE:** 1/2 cup • **PREP TIME:** 10 minutes • **COOK TIME:** 20 minutes + 1 hour chill time

3 medium red potatoes, scrubbed, quartered, and unpeeled

1 hard-cooked egg, finely chopped

1/4 teaspoon salt

Fresh ground pepper

1 teaspoon minced fresh dill or 1/2 teaspoon dried dill

1/4 cup reduced-fat sour cream

1 Boil potatoes for about 20 minutes, until tender yet firm. Drain potatoes and cut into cubes when cool enough to handle. Peel if desired.

2 Toss potatoes with remaining ingredients. Chill for 1 hour.

CHOICES: 2 Starch	**CALORIES FROM FAT:** 20	**CHOLESTEROL:** 60 mg	**DIETARY FIBER:** 2 g
	TOTAL FAT: 2.5 g	**SODIUM:** 185 mg	**SUGARS:** 3 g
	SATURATED FAT: 1.4 g	**POTASSIUM:** 560 mg	**PROTEIN:** 5 g
CALORIES: 150	**TRANS FAT:** 0.0 g	**TOTAL CARBOHYDRATE:** 26 g	**PHOSPHORUS:** 100 mg

MARINATED CUCUMBERS

SERVES: 4 • **SERVING SIZE:** 1/2 cup • **PREP TIME:** 10 minutes • **COOK TIME:** none

1/4 cup vinegar

2 tablespoons water

1/4 teaspoon salt

Dash paprika

Fresh ground pepper to taste

1 medium cucumber, peeled and sliced

1 medium onion, sliced and separated into rings

1 teaspoon fresh parsley, minced

1. Combine all ingredients. Chill, stirring occasionally.

CHOICES: 1 Nonstarchy Vegetable	**CALORIES FROM FAT:** 1	**CHOLESTEROL:** 0 mg	**DIETARY FIBER:** 1 g
	TOTAL FAT: 0 g	**SODIUM:** 148 mg	**SUGARS:** 3 g
	SATURATED FAT: 0.0 g	**POTASSIUM:** 135 mg	**PROTEIN:** 1 g
CALORIES: 22	**TRANS FAT:** 0.0 g	**TOTAL CARBOHYDRATE:** 5 g	**PHOSPHORUS:** 25 mg

CABBAGE FRUIT SLAW

SERVES: 4 • **SERVING SIZE:** 3/4 cup • **PREP TIME:** 10 minutes • **COOK TIME:** none

4 ounces unsweetened pineapple tidbits

2 cups finely shredded cabbage

1 medium unpeeled apple, chopped

3 tablespoons raisins

1 stalk celery, chopped

2 tablespoons reduced-fat mayonnaise

1 tablespoon fat-free plain yogurt

2 tablespoons chopped pecans

1 Drain pineapple, reserving 2 tablespoons juice.

2 Combine pineapple, cabbage, apple, raisins, and celery.

3 Combine reserved juice, mayonnaise, and yogurt, and add to cabbage mixture.

4 Chill. Top with pecans to serve.

CHOICES: 1 Fruit, 1 Fat
CALORIES: 120
CALORIES FROM FAT: 45
TOTAL FAT: 5.0 g
SATURATED FAT: 0.6 g
TRANS FAT: 0.0 g
CHOLESTEROL: 0 mg
SODIUM: 80 mg
POTASSIUM: 250 mg
TOTAL CARBOHYDRATE: 19 g
DIETARY FIBER: 3 g
SUGARS: 14 g
PROTEIN: 2 g
PHOSPHORUS: 45 mg

PICKLED VEGETABLES

SERVES: 26 • **SERVING SIZE:** 1/4 cup • **PREP TIME:** 5 minutes • **COOK TIME:** 10 minutes + 3 days refrigeration time

PICKLING LIQUID

2 cups vinegar, white or cider

2 cups water

1 teaspoon mustard seeds

2 cloves garlic

4 whole cloves

1/2 teaspoon black peppercorns

2 teaspoons thyme

2 teaspoons oregano

4 bay leaves

1/2 teaspoon salt

1 teaspoon sugar

PICKLING VEGETABLES

2 cups sliced carrots

2 cups chopped cauliflower

1 cup julienned green beans

1 cup sweet peas

1 cup cabbage, cut into fine strips

1 cup sliced onion

1–3 small jalapeño peppers (optional)

1 Bring pickling liquid to a boil and boil for 5 minutes, then turn off heat and allow liquid to cool.

2 Meanwhile, blanch the carrots, cauliflower, green beans, and peas in boiling water for 2–3 minutes.

3 If you use jalapeño peppers, cut and remove the seeds and the white vein. Cut into strips.

4 Drain vegetables and place in a glass bowl or container. Add pickling liquid, cabbage, onion, and peppers. Cover and refrigerate at least 3 days before using. Stir occasionally.

CHOICES: 1 Nonstarchy Vegetable
CALORIES: 20
CALORIES FROM FAT: 0
TOTAL FAT: 0.0 g
SATURATED FAT: 0.0 g
TRANS FAT: 0.0 g
CHOLESTEROL: 0 mg
SODIUM: 55 mg
POTASSIUM: 110 mg
TOTAL CARBOHYDRATE: 4 g
DIETARY FIBER: 1 g
SUGARS: 2 g
PROTEIN: 1 g
PHOSPHORUS: 20 mg

POTATO SALAD

SERVES: 12 • **SERVING SIZE:** 2/3 cup • **PREP TIME:** 5 minutes • **COOK TIME:** none

2 pounds red potatoes, peeled, cubed, and cooked

1/4 teaspoon salt

1 small white or yellow onion, peeled and finely chopped

2 hard-boiled eggs, peeled and diced

1 cup frozen peas and carrots, thawed

1 tablespoon extra-virgin olive oil

1–2 teaspoons cider vinegar

1 medium apple, peeled and diced

4 tablespoons reduced-fat mayonnaise

3–4 Spanish-style pimiento strips (optional)

1 Combine all ingredients and mix well. Decorate with pimiento strips, if desired. Serve immediately or chill before serving.

CHOICES: 1 Starch, 1/2 Fat
CALORIES: 110
CALORIES FROM FAT: 30
TOTAL FAT: 3.5 g
SATURATED FAT: 0.7 g
TRANS FAT: 0.0 g
CHOLESTEROL: 35 mg
SODIUM: 115 mg
POTASSIUM: 250 mg
TOTAL CARBOHYDRATE: 17 g
DIETARY FIBER: 2 g
SUGARS: 3 g
PROTEIN: 3 g
PHOSPHORUS: 50 mg

CARROT AND CABBAGE SALAD

SERVES: 4 • **SERVING SIZE:** 1/2 cup • **PREP TIME:** 5 minutes • **COOK TIME:** none

2 cups shredded cabbage

1 small carrot, grated

3 tablespoons fresh lime juice or 1/4 cup vinegar, any type

1/2 teaspoon sugar

1/4 teaspoon salt

1/2 teaspoon black pepper

1 tablespoon chopped cilantro

1–3 tablespoons chopped jalapeño or serrano peppers (optional)

1 Mix all ingredients and toss well.

CHOICES: 1 Nonstarchy Vegetable
CALORIES: 18
CALORIES FROM FAT: 1
TOTAL FAT: 0 g
SATURATED FAT: 0.0 g
TRANS FAT: 0.0 g
CHOLESTEROL: 0 mg
SODIUM: 157 mg
POTASSIUM: 115 mg
TOTAL CARBOHYDRATE: 4 g
DIETARY FIBER: 1 g
SUGARS: 3 g
PROTEIN: 1 g
PHOSPHORUS: 15 mg

GRATED CARROT–RAISIN SALAD

SERVES: 2 • **SERVING SIZE:** 1/3 cup carrot-raisin mixture + 1/4 pear + 1 tablespoon dressing
PREP TIME: 5 minutes • **COOK TIME:** none

1 large carrot, grated
2 tablespoons golden raisins
1/2 large Bartlett pear, peeled and sliced
2 tablespoons fat-free Italian dressing

1 Mix carrot and raisins together. Place mixture in center of plate and surround with pear slices. Drizzle dressing over plate.

CHOICES: 1 Nonstarchy Vegetable, 1 Fruit
CALORIES: 82
CALORIES FROM FAT: 3
TOTAL FAT: 0 g
SATURATED FAT: 0.0 g
TRANS FAT: 0.0 g
CHOLESTEROL: 0 mg
SODIUM: 174 mg
POTASSIUM: 260 mg
TOTAL CARBOHYDRATE: 20 g
DIETARY FIBER: 3 g
SUGARS: 16 g
PROTEIN: 1 g
PHOSPHORUS: 45 mg

BEAN SALAD

SERVES: 6 • **SERVING SIZE:** 1 cup • **PREP TIME:** 10 minutes • **COOK TIME:** 1 hour

1 1/2 cups green beans (fresh or canned)
1 1/2 cups yellow beans (fresh or canned)
1 1/2 cups cooked kidney beans
1/2 cup chopped green pepper
1/2 cup chopped onion

1 clove garlic, minced
2/3 cup red wine vinegar
1 tablespoon artificial sweetener
1/4 cup olive oil
1 teaspoon Worcestershire sauce

1 Blanch green and yellow beans (if using fresh) in rapidly boiling water to cover. Drain. Splash with cold water. Drain again. Mix with kidney beans, peppers, and onions.

2 In a separate bowl, mix remaining dressing ingredients. Toss with beans and let stand 1 hour before serving.

CHOICES: 1/2 Starch, 2 Nonstarchy Vegetable, 2 Fat
CALORIES: 180
CALORIES FROM FAT: 80
TOTAL FAT: 9.0 g
SATURATED FAT: 1.3 g
TRANS FAT: 0.0 g
CHOLESTEROL: 0 mg
SODIUM: 15 mg
POTASSIUM: 330 mg
TOTAL CARBOHYDRATE: 19 g
DIETARY FIBER: 5 g
SUGARS: 4 g
PROTEIN: 5 g
PHOSPHORUS: 90 mg

CUCUMBERS WITH DILL DRESSING

SERVES: 3 • **SERVING SIZE:** 2/3 cup cucumbers and onions + 3 tablespoons dressing + 2 tomato wedges
PREP TIME: 5 minutes • **COOK TIME:** 10 minutes

1/2 cup wine vinegar (can use herbed varieties)
1 tablespoon canola oil
1 teaspoon sugar
1/2 teaspoon dill
1/4 teaspoon fresh ground pepper
1 cup cucumber slices
1 cup thinly sliced red onion rings
1 medium tomato, cut into wedges

1 Combine first five ingredients in a large bowl. Add 1/2 teaspoon salt, if desired.

2 Add vegetables and mix to coat with dressing. Let stand at least 15 minutes before serving.

CHOICES: 2 Nonstarchy Vegetable, 1 Fat
CALORIES: 80
CALORIES FROM FAT: 45
TOTAL FAT: 5 g
SATURATED FAT: 0.0 g
TRANS FAT: 0.0 g
CHOLESTEROL: 0 mg
SODIUM: 6 mg
POTASSIUM: 250 mg
TOTAL CARBOHYDRATE: 9 g
DIETARY FIBER: 2 g
SUGARS: 6 g
PROTEIN: 1 g
PHOSPHORUS: 35 mg

MARINATED BLACK BEANS

SERVES: 10 • **SERVING SIZE:** 1/2 cup • **PREP TIME:** 10 minutes + 3 hours chill time • **COOK TIME:** none

1/3 cup balsamic vinegar
1/3 cup olive oil
3 cloves garlic, crushed
2 15-ounce cans black beans, rinsed and drained
10-ounce package frozen corn, thawed

1 large red pepper, chopped
1 medium green pepper, chopped
1 purple onion, chopped
1 tablespoon chopped fresh cilantro

1 Combine all ingredients, add salt and pepper, if desired, and mix well. Cover and refrigerate 3 hours before serving.

CHOICES: 1 Starch, 1 Nonstarchy Vegetable, 1 1/2 Fat
CALORIES: 170
CALORIES FROM FAT: 70
TOTAL FAT: 8.0 g
SATURATED FAT: 1.1 g
TRANS FAT: 0.0 g
CHOLESTEROL: 0 mg
SODIUM: 65 mg
POTASSIUM: 340 mg
TOTAL CARBOHYDRATE: 22 g
DIETARY FIBER: 6 g
SUGARS: 5 g
PROTEIN: 6 g
PHOSPHORUS: 105 mg

SIDES & SALADS

SPANISH GARBANZO BEANS

SERVES: 2 • **SERVING SIZE:** 1 cup • **PREP TIME:** 5 minutes • **COOK TIME:** 20 minutes

2 tablespoons olive oil
1/2 cup chopped onions
1 medium green pepper, chopped
8 ounces no-added-salt tomato sauce
1 1/4 cups cooked garbanzo beans (chickpeas)
1/4 teaspoon salt

1 In a medium pan, heat olive oil until medium hot. Sauté onions and pepper until onions are translucent. Add tomato sauce. Cook over medium heat 5 minutes.

2 Add garbanzo beans. (If using canned beans, drain and rinse before adding to pan.) Cook over low heat for 15 minutes, stirring occasionally. Add salt.

CHOICES: 2 Starch, 1 Nonstarchy Vegetable, 1 Protein, lean, 2 1/2 Fat
CALORIES: 350
CALORIES FROM FAT: 150
TOTAL FAT: 17.0 g
SATURATED FAT: 2.2 g
TRANS FAT: 0.0 g
CHOLESTEROL: 0 mg
SODIUM: 310 mg
POTASSIUM: 820 mg
TOTAL CARBOHYDRATE: 41 g
DIETARY FIBER: 11 g
SUGARS: 12 g
PROTEIN: 12 g
PHOSPHORUS: 230 mg

COLORFUL RICE

SERVES: 8 • **SERVING SIZE:** 1/2 cup • **PREP TIME:** 5 minutes • **COOK TIME:** 25 minutes

1 tablespoon canola oil
1/4 cup finely chopped onion
1 clove garlic, minced
1 cup long-grain brown rice
1/4 cup finely diced carrots
1/4 cup finely chopped green or red bell pepper
1/4 cup frozen corn
1/4 cup fresh or frozen peas
2 cups low-fat, low-sodium chicken broth
1/4 teaspoon salt
1/8 teaspoon black pepper

1 Heat oil in medium saucepan over medium heat. Sauté onion, garlic, and rice for 4–5 minutes, stirring constantly.

2 Add remaining ingredients and bring to a boil. Reduce heat to low, cover, and simmer 20 minutes or until rice is tender.

CHOICES: 1 1/2 Starch
CALORIES: 120
CALORIES FROM FAT: 20
TOTAL FAT: 2.5 g
SATURATED FAT: 0.3 g
TRANS FAT: 0.0 g
CHOLESTEROL: 0 mg
SODIUM: 115 mg
POTASSIUM: 160 mg
TOTAL CARBOHYDRATE: 21 g
DIETARY FIBER: 1 g
SUGARS: 1 g
PROTEIN: 3 g
PHOSPHORUS: 100 mg

OKLAHOMA BEAN SALAD

SERVES: 10 • **SERVING SIZE:** 1/2 cup • **PREP TIME:** 5 minutes + 2 hours chill time • **COOK TIME:** none

15-ounce can black-eyed peas, rinsed and drained

15-ounce can kidney beans, rinsed and drained

15-ounce can hominy, drained and rinsed

1 cup chopped tomato

2 tablespoons chopped green onion

1 tablespoon chopped garlic

1 jalapeño pepper, chopped (optional)

1 tablespoon lime juice

1/2 cup fat-free Italian dressing

2 teaspoons Italian seasoning

1/4 cup chopped cilantro (optional)

1 Mix all ingredients and refrigerate for at least 2 hours before serving.

CHOICES: 1 1/2 Starch
CALORIES: 100
CALORIES FROM FAT: 5
TOTAL FAT: 0.5 g
SATURATED FAT: 0.2 g
TRANS FAT: 0.0 g
CHOLESTEROL: 0 mg
SODIUM: 270 mg
POTASSIUM: 260 mg
TOTAL CARBOHYDRATE: 19 g
DIETARY FIBER: 5 g
SUGARS: 3 g
PROTEIN: 6 g
PHOSPHORUS: 115 mg

QUICK REFRIED BEANS

SERVES: 5 • **SERVING SIZE:** 1/2 cup • **PREP TIME:** 10 minutes • **COOK TIME:** 30 minutes

1 tablespoon canola oil

1/4 cup chopped onion

2 cloves garlic, minced

1/2 green or red bell pepper, chopped

1/4 teaspoon chili powder

1/4 teaspoon cumin

1/4 teaspoon ground coriander

2 15-ounce cans black beans, rinsed and drained

1 cup low-fat, low-sodium chicken broth

1/2 teaspoon salt

2 tablespoons chopped cilantro (optional)

2 tablespoons chopped onions (optional)

1 Heat oil in a medium skillet over medium-high heat and sauté the onion, garlic, and bell pepper for 3–5 minutes.

2 Add chili powder, cumin, and coriander and sauté 1–2 minutes.

3 Add beans, broth, and salt, and cook 3–5 minutes.

4 Mash beans with a fork or potato masher.

5 Reduce heat to low and cook for 10–15 minutes, stirring several times, until beans are thick. Garnish with cilantro and onions, if desired.

CHOICES: 1 1/2 Starch, 1 Protein, lean
CALORIES: 165
CALORIES FROM FAT: 30
TOTAL FAT: 3.5 g
SATURATED FAT: 0.4 g
TRANS FAT: 0.0 g
CHOLESTEROL: 0 mg
SODIUM: 375 mg
POTASSIUM: 430 mg
TOTAL CARBOHYDRATE: 25 g
DIETARY FIBER: 9 g
SUGARS: 2 g
PROTEIN: 9 g
PHOSPHORUS: 160 mg

BEKAH'S BEET SALAD

SERVES: 6 • **SERVING SIZE:** 1/2 cup • **PREP TIME:** 10 minutes + chill time • **COOK TIME:** none

1 cup canned beets, rinsed, drained, and cubed

2 medium carrots, grated

1 medium tomato, peeled and diced

1/2 cup finely chopped celery

1/4 cup finely chopped cilantro

2 tablespoons lime juice

1/4 teaspoon salt

1/2 clove garlic, minced (optional)

1 Mix all ingredients and toss well.

CHOICES: 1 Nonstarchy Vegetable	**CALORIES FROM FAT:** 2	**CHOLESTEROL:** 0 mg	**DIETARY FIBER:** 2 g
	TOTAL FAT: 0.0 g	**SODIUM:** 177 mg	**SUGARS:** 3 g
	SATURATED FAT: 0.0 g	**POTASSIUM:** 190 mg	**PROTEIN:** 1 g
CALORIES: 25	**TRANS FAT:** 0.0 g	**TOTAL CARBOHYDRATE:** 6 g	**PHOSPHORUS:** 20 mg

CAULIFLOWER SALAD

SERVES: 12 • **SERVING SIZE:** 1/2 cup • **PREP TIME:** 10 minutes • **COOK TIME:** 6–8 minutes + 1 hour chill time

1 medium cauliflower, cut into florets

1/2 cup green beans, fresh (cut in 1-inch pieces), frozen, or canned (rinsed and drained)

1/2 cup fat-free mayonnaise, sour cream, or plain yogurt

2 medium tomatoes, peeled, diced, and drained

1/4 cup grated carrot

1/4 cup finely chopped red onion

1/4 cup chopped red or green bell pepper

1/8–1/4 teaspoon chili powder

2 tablespoons chopped cilantro

1 clove garlic, minced

1/4 teaspoon salt

1/4 teaspoon black pepper

1 teaspoon fresh lime juice

1 cup shredded lettuce

1 Cook cauliflower and green beans (if fresh or frozen) in boiling water for 6–8 minutes. Drain.

2 Meanwhile, combine remaining ingredients except lettuce and mix well. Toss with vegetables and lettuce and refrigerate at least 1 hour before serving.

CHOICES: 1 Nonstarchy Vegetable	**CALORIES FROM FAT:** 0	**CHOLESTEROL:** 0 mg	**DIETARY FIBER:** 2 g
	TOTAL FAT: 0.0 g	**SODIUM:** 135 mg	**SUGARS:** 3 g
	SATURATED FAT: 0.1 g	**POTASSIUM:** 240 mg	**PROTEIN:** 1 g
CALORIES: 30	**TRANS FAT:** 0.0 g	**TOTAL CARBOHYDRATE:** 6 g	**PHOSPHORUS:** 35 mg

SWEET PEPPER, ONION, AND TOMATO SALAD

SERVES: 6 • **SERVING SIZE:** 2/3 cup tomato and pepper + 2 tomato wedges + 2 tablespoons dressing
PREP TIME: 10 minutes + 8 hours chill time • **COOK TIME:** none

1/2 cup cider vinegar
2 teaspoons fresh lime juice
1 tablespoon extra-virgin olive oil
3 tablespoons chopped cilantro
1 clove garlic, sliced
1 teaspoon sugar
1/4 teaspoon salt
1/2 teaspoon black pepper

1 tablespoon ketchup
1 teaspoon Worcestershire sauce
1 large bell pepper, any color, cut into thin rings
1 large onion, sliced into thin rings
2 large tomatoes, peeled, cut into 6 wedges each

1 Combine all ingredients except peppers, onion, and tomato. Mix well. Pour dressing over vegetables and stir.

2 Cover and refrigerate for several hours or overnight, stirring occasionally.

CHOICES: 2 Nonstarchy Vegetable, 1/2 Fat	**CALORIES FROM FAT:** 21	**CHOLESTEROL:** 0 mg	**DIETARY FIBER:** 2 g
	TOTAL FAT: 2.0 g	**SODIUM:** 145 mg	**SUGARS:** 6 g
	SATURATED FAT: 0.0 g	**POTASSIUM:** 290 mg	**PROTEIN:** 1 g
CALORIES: 63	**TRANS FAT:** 0.0 g	**TOTAL CARBOHYDRATE:** 10 g	**PHOSPHORUS:** 35 mg

BEET SALAD

SERVES: 6 • **SERVING SIZE:** 1/2 cup • **PREP TIME:** 10 minutes • **COOK TIME:** none

2 cups cooked or canned sliced beets, drained
1/4 cup sliced onions
2 tablespoons red wine vinegar
1/2 teaspoon Dijon mustard
1/4 cup olive oil

1 Combine beets and onions in a bowl. Whisk together vinegar, mustard, and oil. Pour over vegetables. Refrigerate and serve.

CHOICES: 1 Nonstarchy Vegetable, 2 Fat	**CALORIES FROM FAT:** 80	**CHOLESTEROL:** 0 mg	**DIETARY FIBER:** 1 g
	TOTAL FAT: 9.0 g	**SODIUM:** 120 mg	**SUGARS:** 3 g
	SATURATED FAT: 1.3 g	**POTASSIUM:** 100 mg	**PROTEIN:** 1 g
CALORIES: 100	**TRANS FAT:** 0.0 g	**TOTAL CARBOHYDRATE:** 5 g	**PHOSPHORUS:** 10 mg

SUNFLOWER SEED COLESLAW

SERVES: 8 • **SERVING SIZE:** 1 cup • **PREP TIME:** 5 minutes • **COOK TIME:** 3 minutes

1/4 cup sunflower seeds

2 tablespoons sesame seeds

8 cups cabbage, grated fine

1/2 cup finely chopped red bell pepper

3 tablespoons canola oil

2 teaspoons lemon juice

1 tablespoon cider vinegar

1 teaspoon honey

1 teaspoon artificial sweetener

1 Roast sunflower and sesame seeds in a dry skillet or toaster oven over medium heat. Stir or shake often. Seeds will brown and start to pop in about 2–3 minutes. Remove from heat.

2 Mix seeds with remaining ingredients. Add salt and pepper, if desired. For best flavor, make a day or two in advance and refrigerate.

CHOICES: 2 Nonstarchy Vegetable, 1 1/2 Fat	**CALORIES FROM FAT:** 78	**CHOLESTEROL:** 0 mg	**DIETARY FIBER:** 3 g
	TOTAL FAT: 8.0 g	**SODIUM:** 17 mg	**SUGARS:** 4 g
	SATURATED FAT: 0.8 g	**POTASSIUM:** 220 mg	**PROTEIN:** 3 g
CALORIES: 113	**TRANS FAT:** 0.0 g	**TOTAL CARBOHYDRATE:** 8 g	**PHOSPHORUS:** 85 mg

SAUTÉED KALE AND ONION

SERVES: 4 • **SERVING SIZE:** 1 cup • **PREP TIME:** 5 minutes • **COOK TIME:** 8 minutes

1 large chopped onion

Nonstick cooking spray

1 large bunch kale, cleaned and chopped

1/4 cup water

1 tablespoon lemon juice

1 Sauté onion in nonstick skillet sprayed with cooking spray until translucent, about 3–5 minutes.

2 Add remaining ingredients. Sauté 2–3 more minutes. Serve immediately.

CHOICES: 2 Nonstarchy Vegetable	**CALORIES FROM FAT:** 0	**CHOLESTEROL:** 0 mg	**DIETARY FIBER:** 2 g
	TOTAL FAT: 0.0 g	**SODIUM:** 20 mg	**SUGARS:** 3 g
	SATURATED FAT: 0.1 g	**POTASSIUM:** 250 mg	**PROTEIN:** 2g
CALORIES: 45	**TRANS FAT:** 0.0 g	**TOTAL CARBOHYDRATE:** 10 g	**PHOSPHORUS:** 35 mg

ASIAN SLAW

SERVES: 8 • **SERVING SIZE:** 1 1/2 cups • **PREP TIME:** 10 minutes + 2 hours refrigeration time • **COOK TIME:** none

8 cups shredded green cabbage
2 cups shredded red cabbage
1 cup shredded carrot
1 peeled, seeded, and chopped cucumber
1/4 cup chopped green onion

1/3 cup chopped fresh cilantro
2 tablespoons sesame oil
1/4 cup rice vinegar
1 tablespoon lime juice
2 tablespoons lite soy sauce
1 tablespoon minced garlic

1 teaspoon ground ginger
1 teaspoon sugar
12 ounces (3/4 pound) firm tofu, drained and cubed

1 Toss cabbages, carrots, cucumber, onion, and cilantro together in salad bowl.

2 Whisk together sesame oil, vinegar, lime juice, soy sauce, garlic, ginger, and sugar. Pour dressing over vegetables, add tofu, and toss.

3 Refrigerate at least 2 hours or up to 24 hours. Serve over steamed brown rice or stuffed into pita bread.

CHOICES: 2 Nonstarchy Vegetable, 1 Fat
CALORIES: 95
CALORIES FROM FAT: 45
TOTAL FAT: 5.0 g
SATURATED FAT: 1.0 g
TRANS FAT: 0.0 g
CHOLESTEROL: 0 mg
SODIUM: 189 mg
POTASSIUM: 340 mg
TOTAL CARBOHYDRATE: 10 g
DIETARY FIBER: 3 g
SUGARS: 6 g
PROTEIN: 5 g
PHOSPHORUS: 80 mg

RAINBOW RICE

SERVES: 4 • **SERVING SIZE:** 1 cup • **PREP TIME:** 5 minutes • **COOK TIME:** 5 minutes

1 cup black beans, rinsed and drained
1/2 cup frozen corn kernels
1/2 cup frozen green peas
2 cups cooked long-grain brown rice
2 tablespoons chopped onion

1 Heat beans, corn, and peas in the microwave or on the stovetop. Combine all ingredients. Serve hot.

CHOICES: 2 1/2 Starch
CALORIES: 200
CALORIES FROM FAT: 15
TOTAL FAT: 1.5 g
SATURATED FAT: 0.3 g
TRANS FAT: 0.0 g
CHOLESTEROL: 0 mg
SODIUM: 70 mg
POTASSIUM: 300 mg
TOTAL CARBOHYDRATE: 41 g
DIETARY FIBER: 7 g
SUGARS: 3 g
PROTEIN: 8 g
PHOSPHORUS: 185 mg

CRANBERRY WILD RICE STUFFING

SERVES: 4 • **SERVING SIZE:** 1/2 cup • **PREP TIME:** 10 minutes • **COOK TIME:** 2 hours

1 1/2 cups water
1/2 cup wild rice, rinsed
1/4 cup dark or golden raisins
1 tablespoon canola oil
5 green onions, sliced
1/2 cup sliced celery or fennel bulb
1 cup fresh or frozen cranberries, slightly thawed
1 teaspoon grated orange rind
1/2 teaspoon dried thyme

1 In a heavy saucepan, bring water to a boil. Add rice and raisins, and return to a boil. Reduce heat and summer for 50–60 minutes, until rice is tender.

2 In a large skillet over medium-high heat, heat the oil. Add onions and celery. Sauté for 3 minutes. Add cranberries, orange rind, thyme, and cooked rice.

3 Preheat oven to 350°F. Stuff rice mixture into two Cornish hens, 3-pound chicken, or use with turkey breast. (Stuffing can alternatively be placed into a casserole dish and baked for 40 minutes.) Bake for 1 hour or until the poultry is tender and juices run clear.

CHOICES: 1 Starch, 1/2 Fruit, 1/2 Fat	**CALORIES FROM FAT:** 35	**CHOLESTEROL:** 0 mg	**DIETARY FIBER:** 3 g
	TOTAL FAT: 4.0 g	**SODIUM:** 15 mg	**SUGARS:** 7 g
	SATURATED FAT: 0.3 g	**POTASSIUM:** 240 mg	**PROTEIN:** 3 g
CALORIES: 145	**TRANS FAT:** 0.0 g	**TOTAL CARBOHYDRATE:** 26 g	**PHOSPHORUS:** 75 mg

BROILED MUSHROOM CAPS

SERVES: 4 • **SERVING SIZE:** 4 mushroom caps • **PREP TIME:** 10 minutes • **COOK TIME:** 10 minutes

1 pound large fresh mushrooms, cleaned
Nonstick cooking spray
1 tablespoon tub margarine (30–50% vegetable oil)
1 tablespoon canola oil
2 teaspoon minced garlic
2 tablespoons lemon juice
1 tablespoon freshly grated Parmesan cheese

1 Set oven to broil. Remove stems from mushrooms and reserve for use in a meatloaf or omelet. Arrange caps in a pan sprayed with nonstick cooking spray.

2 Broil for 2 minutes. Turn mushrooms over and broil 2 more minutes.

3. Meanwhile, melt margarine with oil in a saucepan. Add garlic and lemon juice. Pour over mushrooms in a serving dish. Sprinkle with cheese.

CHOICES: 1 Nonstarchy Vegetable, 1 Fat	**CALORIES FROM FAT:** 45	**CHOLESTEROL:** 0 mg	**DIETARY FIBER:** 2 g
	TOTAL FAT: 5.0 g	**SODIUM:** 35 mg	**SUGARS:** 2 g
	SATURATED FAT: 0.8 g	**POTASSIUM:** 280 mg	**PROTEIN:** 2 g
CALORIES: 70	**TRANS FAT:** 0.0 g	**TOTAL CARBOHYDRATE:** 5 g	**PHOSPHORUS:** 75 mg

BRUSSELS SPROUTS WITH WALNUTS

SERVES: 4 • **SERVING SIZE:** 1/2 cup • **PREP TIME:** 10 minutes • **COOK TIME:** 20 minutes

2 cups fresh Brussels sprouts

1 tablespoon tub margarine (30–50% vegetable oil)

1/4 cup chopped walnuts or pecans

1/4 teaspoon ground nutmeg

1 Trim off the end of each Brussels sprout, then cut in half.

2 In a saucepan with 1 inch of water, place a steamer basket. Place all sprouts in the steamer, cover pan, and steam on high heat for 15 minutes, until sprouts are tender.

3 Meanwhile, in a small skillet over medium-high heat, melt the margarine. Add walnuts and sauté for 3 minutes until golden brown.

4 Place sprouts in a serving dish. Pour walnuts on top. Sprinkle with nutmeg and season with pepper and salt, if desired.

CHOICES: 1 Nonstarchy Vegetable, 1 1/2 Fat	**CALORIES FROM FAT:** 65	**CHOLESTEROL:** 0 mg	**DIETARY FIBER:** 3 g
	TOTAL FAT: 7.0 g	**SODIUM:** 40 mg	**SUGARS:** 2 g
	SATURATED FAT: 0.8 g	**POTASSIUM:** 280 mg	**PROTEIN:** 3 g
CALORIES: 90	**TRANS FAT:** 0.0 g	**TOTAL CARBOHYDRATE:** 7 g	**PHOSPHORUS:** 70 mg

HEALTHY POTATO SALAD

SERVES: 5 • **SERVING SIZE:** 2/3 cup • **PREP TIME:** 5 minutes • **COOK TIME:** 8–10 minutes

2 medium potatoes

1 hard-boiled egg

1/4 cup chopped celery

1/4 cup chopped green pepper

1/4 cup chopped sweet onion or scallions

2 tablespoons chopped pimiento

1 tablespoon prepared mustard

3 tablespoons fat-free salad dressing or mayonnaise

1 Cut potatoes into small 1/2-inch cubes, leaving skin on. Boil in lightly salted water until tender but still intact (8–10 minutes). Drain.

2 Combine rest of ingredients and add to potatoes; lightly mix. Refrigerate until served.

	CALORIES FROM FAT: 15	**CHOLESTEROL:** 45 mg	**DIETARY FIBER:** 2 g
	TOTAL FAT: 1.5 g	**SODIUM:** 130 mg	**SUGARS:** 2 g
CHOICES: 1 Starch	**SATURATED FAT:** 0.4 g	**POTASSIUM:** 300 mg	**PROTEIN:** 3 g
CALORIES: 90	**TRANS FAT:** 0.0 g	**TOTAL CARBOHYDRATE:** 17 g	**PHOSPHORUS:** 60 mg

ROGER'S COLESLAW

SERVES: 8 • **SERVING SIZE:** 1/2 cup • **PREP TIME:** 5 minutes • **COOK TIME:** none

1 pound head of green cabbage, shredded

1 medium cucumber, peeled and chopped

1/2 cup fat-free mayonnaise

1 tablespoon vinegar

2–3 packets artificial sweetener

Fresh ground pepper to taste

1 teaspoon celery seed

1 Combine all ingredients. Add salt, if desired. Refrigerate until served.

CHOICES: 1 Nonstarchy Vegetable	**CALORIES FROM FAT:** 1	**CHOLESTEROL:** 0 mg	**DIETARY FIBER:** 1 g
	TOTAL FAT: 0.0 g	**SODIUM:** 123 mg	**SUGARS:** 3 g
	SATURATED FAT: 0.0 g	**POTASSIUM:** 130 mg	**PROTEIN:** 1 g
CALORIES: 28	**TRANS FAT:** 0.0 g	**TOTAL CARBOHYDRATE:** 6 g	**PHOSPHORUS:** 25 mg

FRESH TOMATO AND BASIL SALAD

SERVES: 4 • **SERVING SIZE:** 1 tomato + 3 1/2 tablespoons marinade • **PREP TIME:** 10 minutes + chill time • **COOK TIME:** none

3/4 cup red wine vinegar

1 tablespoon olive oil

1/4 teaspoon garlic powder

Fresh ground pepper to taste

1/2 cup fresh basil, chopped

4 tomatoes

1 Whisk together vinegar, oil, garlic powder, pepper, and basil. Add 1/4 teaspoon salt, if desired.

2 Cut each tomato into 4 wedges and pour dressing over them. Marinate tomatoes for 3–4 hours.

CHOICES: 2 Nonstarchy Vegetable, 1/2 Fat	**CALORIES FROM FAT:** 30	**CHOLESTEROL:** 0 mg	**DIETARY FIBER:** 2 g
	TOTAL FAT: 3.5 g	**SODIUM:** 10 mg	**SUGARS:** 5 g
	SATURATED FAT: 0.5 g	**POTASSIUM:** 390 mg	**PROTEIN:** 1 g
CALORIES: 65	**TRANS FAT:** 0.0 g	**TOTAL CARBOHYDRATE:** 8 g	**PHOSPHORUS:** 45 mg

MIXED-FIBER PILAF

SERVES: 10 • **SERVING SIZE:** 1/3 cup • **PREP TIME:** 5 minutes • **COOK TIME:** 25 minutes

2 teaspoons olive oil
1/2 cup chopped onion
1/2 cup thinly sliced mushrooms
1/3 cup bulgur wheat
1/2 cup quick-cooking brown rice
1/4 quick-cooking barley
1 1/2 cups defatted chicken broth or water
1/8 teaspoon thyme
Fresh ground pepper to taste

1 Heat oil in a large skillet and sauté onions and mushrooms until onions are translucent and all liquid is gone.

2 Add bulgur, rice, and barley and continue to sauté until lightly golden brown.

3 Add chicken broth and simmer, covered, on low for 15 minutes or until grains are tender and liquid has been absorbed. Season with thyme and pepper before serving.

CHOICES: 1 Starch	**CALORIES FROM FAT:** 10	**CHOLESTEROL:** 0 mg	**DIETARY FIBER:** 2 g
	TOTAL FAT: 1.0 g	**SODIUM:** 80 mg	**SUGARS:** 1 g
CALORIES: 70	**SATURATED FAT:** 0.2 g	**POTASSIUM:** 100 mg	**PROTEIN:** 2 g
	TRANS FAT: 0.0 g	**TOTAL CARBOHYDRATE:** 13 g	**PHOSPHORUS:** 60 mg

WHOLE-WHEAT BREAD OR ROLLS

SERVES: 36 • **SERVING SIZE:** 1 slice or roll • **PREP TIME:** 1 hour 15 minutes • **COOK TIME:** 35–45 minutes

2 tablespoons dry yeast
3 cups warm water
1/2 cup canola oil

1/2 cup molasses
2 teaspoons salt
1 beaten egg

8 cups whole-wheat flour

1 Sprinkle yeast into warm water and stir until dissolved.

2 Add oil, molasses, salt, and egg. Blend well.

3 Add half of the flour and beat until smooth. Work the remaining flour in with hands.

4 Turn dough out onto a lightly floured board and knead until smooth and elastic, at least 10 minutes.

5 Place in an oiled bowl and turn to oil all sides of the dough. Cover with a hand towel. Set in a warm setting, free from drafts, until double in size (approximately 1 hour).

6 Punch down and divide into thirds. Shape into loaves. Place in oiled pans and let rise in a warm place until double in size. Can also form into rolls and let rise on a baking sheet.

7 Heat oven to 400°F. Bake 15 minutes for rolls or 35–45 minutes for bread. Remove from pans and set on racks to cool.

CHOICES: 1 1/2 Starch, 1/2 Fat	**CALORIES FROM FAT:** 34	**CHOLESTEROL:** 6 mg	**DIETARY FIBER:** 3 g
	TOTAL FAT: 4.0 g	**SODIUM:** 134 mg	**SUGARS:** 3 g
	SATURATED FAT: 0.4 g	**POTASSIUM:** 180 mg	**PROTEIN:** 4 g
CALORIES: 134	**TRANS FAT:** 0.0 g	**TOTAL CARBOHYDRATE:** 23 g	**PHOSPHORUS:** 105 mg

LIGHTLY SCALLOPED POTATOES

SERVES: 8 • **SERVING SIZE:** 1/2 cup • **PREP TIME:** 10 minutes • **COOK TIME:** 50 minutes + 20 minutes stand time

Nonstick cooking spray
1/4 cup diced onion
1 clove garlic, minced
2 1/2 teaspoons flour
6 ounces evaporated fat-free milk
3/4 cup fat-free milk
1/4 teaspoon salt
1/4 teaspoon cayenne pepper
4 1/2 cups thinly sliced red potatoes, rinsed and drained
1/2 cup shredded reduced-fat cheddar or Swiss cheese
1/4 cup freshly grated Parmesan cheese

1 Preheat oven to 350°F.
2 Spray a nonstick saucepan with cooking spray and sauté onion and garlic until tender. Add flour and mix well. Add evaporated milk, milk, salt, and cayenne pepper. Cook until slightly thickened, stirring constantly, about 2 minutes.
3 Alternate layers of potato, cheeses, and sauce in 2-quart baking dish that has been coated with cooking spray.
4 Bake for 45 minutes or until bubbly and golden brown. Let stand 20 minutes before serving.

CHOICES: 1 1/2 Starch, 1/2 Fat
CALORIES: 140
CALORIES FROM FAT: 20
TOTAL FAT: 2.5 g
SATURATED FAT: 1.3 g
TRANS FAT: 0.0 g
CHOLESTEROL: 5 mg
SODIUM: 210 mg
POTASSIUM: 470 mg
TOTAL CARBOHYDRATE: 23 g
DIETARY FIBER: 2 g
SUGARS: 5 g
PROTEIN: 7 g
PHOSPHORUS: 170 mg

TRADITIONAL BREAD DRESSING

SERVES: 8 • **SERVING SIZE:** 1/2 cup • **PREP TIME:** 5 minutes • **COOK TIME:** 30–40 minutes

4 cups whole-wheat bread cubes, crusts removed
1 cup chopped celery
1/3 cup chopped onion
1 tablespoon minced fresh parsley
1 garlic clove, minced
1/2 cup hot water or low-sodium, low-fat chicken broth
1/4 teaspoon ground sage
1/4 teaspoon ground marjoram
1/4 teaspoon ground thyme
1/4 teaspoon dried basil
Nonstick cooking spray

1 Preheat oven to 350°F. Combine all ingredients in a large bowl. Add salt and pepper, if desired.
2 Place the mixture in a casserole dish sprayed with nonstick cooking spray. Bake covered for 30–40 minutes.

CHOICES: 1/2 Starch
CALORIES: 50
CALORIES FROM FAT: 5
TOTAL FAT: 0.5 g
SATURATED FAT: 0.1 g
TRANS FAT: 0.0 g
CHOLESTEROL: 0 mg
SODIUM: 90 mg
POTASSIUM: 90 mg
TOTAL CARBOHYDRATE: 9 g
DIETARY FIBER: 1 g
SUGARS: 1 g
PROTEIN: 2 g
PHOSPHORUS: 45 mg

GREG'S GAZPACHO

SERVES: 12 • **SERVING SIZE:** 2/3 cup • **PREP TIME:** 10 minutes • **COOK TIME:** 30–45 minutes + 2 hours chill time

2 cups tomatoes, peeled, seeded, and chopped
1 cup peeled, cubed cucumber
1/2 green pepper, chopped
1/2 cup red onion, chopped
1/4 cup green onion, sliced
4 cups V-8 juice
1 tablespoon lemon juice
Hot pepper sauce to taste

1 To peel and seed tomatoes, bring a small pan of water to a boil. With a sharp knife, cut an X on the bottom of each tomato. Put in 1 whole fresh tomato so that water covers the entire tomato. Leave in water 30–45 seconds. Remove tomato and immediately run under cold water, peeling skin at the X. Cut in half and squeeze gently to remove seeds.

2 Set aside 1/4 of the raw, chopped, and sliced vegetables to garnish the soup. Add the remaining vegetables to the juices and refrigerate 2 hours. If soup is chunkier than desired, it can be blended slightly.

3 Serve cold with abundant garnishes.

CHOICES: 1 Nonstarchy Vegetable
CALORIES: 25
CALORIES FROM FAT: 0
TOTAL FAT: 0.0 g
SATURATED FAT: 0.0 g
TRANS FAT: 0.0 g
CHOLESTEROL: 0 mg
SODIUM: 140 mg
POTASSIUM: 270 mg
TOTAL CARBOHYDRATE: 6 g
DIETARY FIBER: 1 g
SUGARS: 4 g
PROTEIN: 1 g
PHOSPHORUS: 25 mg

FIG, CRANBERRY, AND ALMOND ENERGY BITES

SERVES: 24 • **SERVING SIZE:** 1 bite • **PREP TIME:** 15 minutes • **COOK TIME:** none

1 cup chopped dried figs
1 cup natural almonds
1 cup dried, unsweetened cranberries
1 cup unsweetened coconut flakes
5 ounces honey
1 teaspoon cinnamon
1 cup oatmeal

1 Place all ingredients in a food processor with steel blade. Process until finely chopped and well blended.

2 Form into 24 balls and place in an airtight container in the refrigerator.

CHOICES: 1 Carbohydrate, 1 Fat
CALORIES: 110
CALORIES FROM FAT: 45
TOTAL FAT: 5.0 g
SATURATED FAT: 2.2 g
TRANS FAT: 0.0 g
CHOLESTEROL: 0 mg
SODIUM: 0 mg
POTASSIUM: 120 mg
TOTAL CARBOHYDRATE: 15 g
DIETARY FIBER: 3 g
SUGARS: 9 g
ADDED SUGARS: 5 g
PROTEIN: 2 g
PHOSPHORUS: 55 mg

SAVORY SPICED WALNUTS

SERVES: 8 • **SERVING SIZE:** 1/4 cup • **PREP TIME:** 10 minutes • **COOK TIME:** 20 minutes

1/4 teaspoon ground turmeric

1 1/2 teaspoons ground cinnamon

1/4 teaspoon ground allspice

1 egg white

2 cups walnut halves or pecan halves

1/2 cup old fashioned oats

1. Preheat oven to 350°F.
2. Combine spices in a small bowl; set aside.
3. Beat egg white until foamy (soft peaks will form) in a medium bowl.
4. Add walnuts, oats, and spice mixture. Toss to coat nuts evenly.
5. Spread nuts on a parchment-lined baking sheet in a single layer. Bake 20 minutes or until golden brown and crispy. Cool completely and store in an airtight container up to 2 weeks.

CHOICES: 1/2 Carbohydrate, 1 Protein, lean, 3 Fat
CALORIES: 200
CALORIES FROM FAT: 160
TOTAL FAT: 18.0 g
SATURATED FAT: 1.7 g
TRANS FAT: 0.0 g
CHOLESTEROL: 0 mg
SODIUM: 10 mg
POTASSIUM: 150 mg
TOTAL CARBOHYDRATE: 8 g
DIETARY FIBER: 3 g
SUGARS: 1 g
ADDED SUGARS: 0 g
PROTEIN: 5 g
PHOSPHORUS: 115 mg

ITALIAN ROASTED CHICKPEAS

SERVES: 6 • **SERVING SIZE:** 1/4 cup • **PREP TIME:** 10 minutes • **COOK TIME:** 25 minutes

1 1/2 cups canned chickpeas (15-ounce can)

1 tablespoon extra virgin olive oil

2 teaspoons Italian seasoning blend, no salt added

1. Preheat oven to 400°F convection.
2. Drain and rinse the chickpeas. Place on paper towels to dry.
3. Place chickpeas, olive oil, and seasoning in an 8-inch baking dish. Mix well.
4. Roast 25 minutes or until desired crispness.
5. Cool and store in an airtight container.

CHOICES: 1 Starch, 1/2 Fat
CALORIES: 90
CALORIES FROM FAT: 30
TOTAL FAT: 3.5 g
SATURATED FAT: 0.4 g
TRANS FAT: 0.0 g
CHOLESTEROL: 0 mg
SODIUM: 70 mg
POTASSIUM: 125 mg
TOTAL CARBOHYDRATE: 12 g
DIETARY FIBER: 3 g
SUGARS: 2 g
ADDED SUGARS: 0 g
PROTEIN: 4 g
PHOSPHORUS: 70 mg

RECIPE PHOTO ON PREVIOUS PAGE:
Crab Cake, pg. 121

FRENCH DRESSING

SERVES: 6 • **SERVING SIZE:** 2 tablespoons • **PREP TIME:** 5 minutes • **COOK TIME:** none

1/2 cup tomato or V-8 juice

2 tablespoons lemon juice or white wine vinegar

1 tablespoon finely chopped onion

1 tablespoon finely chopped green pepper

1 teaspoon minced garlic

1/4 teaspoon salt

Fresh ground pepper

1 Combine all ingredients in jar with lid. Cover and shake well before using. Store in refrigerator for up to two months.

CHOICES: Free Food
CALORIES: 6

CALORIES FROM FAT: 0
TOTAL FAT: 0 g
SATURATED FAT: 0.0 g
TRANS FAT: 0.0 g

CHOLESTEROL: 0 mg
SODIUM: 150 mg
POTASSIUM: 60 mg
TOTAL CARBOHYDRATE: 2 g

DIETARY FIBER: 0 g
SUGARS: 1 g
PROTEIN: 0 g
PHOSPHORUS: 5 mg

CRANBERRY-RAISIN DRESSING

SERVES: 4 • **SERVING SIZE:** 1/4 cup • **PREP TIME:** 5 minutes • **COOK TIME:** 15 minutes + 20–30 minutes chill time

1 cup orange juice

1/2 cup fresh or frozen cranberries, slightly thawed

1/8 teaspoon ground cloves

4 tablespoons dark or golden raisins

1 stick cinnamon

2 teaspoons cornstarch

1 packet sugar substitute

1 Combine juice and cranberries in a saucepan. Cook over medium heat just until the berries pop.

2 Add cloves, raisins, and cinnamon stick and reduce heat to medium low, stirring frequently for about 5 minutes.

3 Turn heat off and add cornstarch. Stir for 1 minute. Add sugar substitute.

4 Pour into a container and let cool for 20–30 minutes in the refrigerator, or serve warm.

CHOICES: 1 Fruit
CALORIES: 67

CALORIES FROM FAT: 1
TOTAL FAT: 0 g
SATURATED FAT: 0.0 g
TRANS FAT: 0.0 g

CHOLESTEROL: 0 mg
SODIUM: 2 mg
POTASSIUM: 200 mg
TOTAL CARBOHYDRATE: 17 g

DIETARY FIBER: 1 g
SUGARS: 14 g
PROTEIN: 1 g
PHOSPHORUS: 20 mg

MASTOKHIAR

SERVES: 2 • **SERVING SIZE:** 1 cup • **PREP TIME:** 5 minutes + 1–2 hours chill time • **COOK TIME:** none

1 1/2 cups low-fat plain yogurt

1 cucumber, peeled and finely chopped

1/4 cup raisins

1/8 teaspoon salt

1/2 teaspoon dried or 1/2 tablespoon chopped fresh mint leaves

1 Mix all ingredients. Chill 1–2 hours before serving.

CHOICES: 1 Fruit, 1 Milk, fat-free, 1 Nonstarchy Vegetable
CALORIES: 180

CALORIES FROM FAT: 25
TOTAL FAT: 3.0 g
SATURATED FAT: 1.9 g
TRANS FAT: 0.0 g

CHOLESTEROL: 10 mg
SODIUM: 265 mg
POTASSIUM: 680 mg
TOTAL CARBOHYDRATE: 29 g

DIETARY FIBER: 1 g
SUGARS: 24 g
PROTEIN: 10 g
PHOSPHORUS: 305 mg

SOFRITO

SERVES: 32 • **SERVING SIZE:** 1 tablespoon • **PREP TIME:** 5 minutes • **COOK TIME:** none

1 small peeled onion

1/2 medium red bell pepper, seeds removed

1/2 medium green bell pepper, seeds removed

1 tomato, seeded

1/2 Caribbean culantro leaf

1 tablespoon fresh cilantro

1 Blend all ingredients until mixture is soft, then store in refrigerator.

CHOICES: Free Food
CALORIES: 3

CALORIES FROM FAT: 0
TOTAL FAT: 0 g
SATURATED FAT: 0.0 g
TRANS FAT: 0.0 g

CHOLESTEROL: 0 mg
SODIUM: 1 mg
POTASSIUM: 25 mg
TOTAL CARBOHYDRATE: 1 g

DIETARY FIBER: 0 g
SUGARS: 0 g
PROTEIN: 0 g
PHOSPHORUS: 0 mg

RANCHERA SAUCE

SERVES: 14 • **SERVING SIZE:** 1/4 cup • **PREP TIME:** 10 minutes • **COOK TIME:** none

6 medium tomatoes, roasted, skinned, and seeded

1–2 hot red chilies (Fresno, jalapeño, serrano, or New Mexican red)

2 medium onions, peeled and cut into chunks

1–2 cloves garlic, peeled

1 tablespoon fresh cilantro

1/2 teaspoon sugar

1/2 teaspoon salt

1 tablespoon white or apple cider vinegar

1 tablespoon fresh parsley

1 Combine all ingredients in a blender or food processor. Blend until the sauce is smooth.

CHOICES: 1 Nonstarchy Vegetable
CALORIES: 20

CALORIES FROM FAT: 2
TOTAL FAT: 0 g
SATURATED FAT: 0.0 g
TRANS FAT: 0.0 g

CHOLESTEROL: 0 mg
SODIUM: 88 mg
POTASSIUM: 150 mg
TOTAL CARBOHYDRATE: 5 g

DIETARY FIBER: 1 g
SUGARS: 3 g
PROTEIN: 1 g
PHOSPHORUS: 20 mg

FRESH SALSA

SERVES: 14 • **SERVING SIZE:** 1/4 cup • **PREP TIME:** 5 minutes + 30 minutes stand time • **COOK TIME:** none

3 large tomatoes, peeled and diced

1/2 cup finely chopped white onion

1/2 jalapeño pepper, seeded, deveined, and chopped

1 Anaheim pepper, seeded, deveined, and chopped

1/2 red bell pepper, chopped

2 tablespoons chopped cilantro

1/2 teaspoon salt

Fresh juice from 1/2 lime

1 teaspoon white wine vinegar

1 tablespoon water or tomato juice

1 Combine all ingredients, mix well, and let stand for 30 minutes.

CHOICES: Free Food
CALORIES: 16

CALORIES FROM FAT: 2
TOTAL FAT: 0 g
SATURATED FAT: 0.0 g
TRANS FAT: 0.0 g

CHOLESTEROL: 0 mg
SODIUM: 88 mg
POTASSIUM: 140 mg
TOTAL CARBOHYDRATE: 4 g

DIETARY FIBER: 1 g
SUGARS: 2 g
PROTEIN: 1 g
PHOSPHORUS: 15 mg

HUMMUS

SERVES: 6 • **SERVING SIZE:** 1/3 cup • **PREP TIME:** 5 minutes • **COOK TIME:** none

2 cups cooked or canned
    garbanzo beans (chickpeas),
    drained (reserve 1/2 cup liquid)
1 clove garlic
1 tablespoon sesame tahini
2 tablespoons olive oil
1 whole roasted red pepper,
    seeded (available in jars)
1 tablespoon lemon juice

1 Blend all ingredients in a
   blender or food processor.

CHOICES: 1 Starch, 1 Protein, lean, 1 Fat
CALORIES: 155

CALORIES FROM FAT: 65
TOTAL FAT: 7.0 g
SATURATED FAT: 1.0 g
TRANS FAT: 0.0 g

CHOLESTEROL: 0 mg
SODIUM: 55 mg
POTASSIUM: 210 mg
TOTAL CARBOHYDRATE: 17 g

DIETARY FIBER: 5 g
SUGARS: 3 g
PROTEIN: 6 g
PHOSPHORUS: 115 mg

CLAM SAUCE

SERVES: 5 • **SERVING SIZE:** 1 cup • **PREP TIME:** 5 minutes • **COOK TIME:** 15 minutes

2 teaspoons olive oil
1 cup chopped onion
1/2 green pepper, chopped
1 1/2 cups sliced mushrooms
2 cloves garlic, minced
3 10-ounce cans whole baby
    clams with liquid
1 1/2 cups fresh tomatoes,
    peeled, seeded, and diced
1/4 cup fat-free half and half
Fresh ground pepper to taste
1/2 cup freshly grated
    Parmesan cheese

1 Heat skillet and add olive
   oil. Sauté onion, pepper,
   mushrooms, and garlic.
2 Add clams and liquid.
   Simmer to reduce liquid by
   1/3 to 1/2.

3 Add tomatoes and half and
   half. Simmer until large
   glossy bubbles form.
4 Season with pepper and
   toss with grated cheese.
   Serve over cooked pasta.

CHOICES: 1 Carbohydrate, 3 Protein, lean
CALORIES: 210

CALORIES FROM FAT: 65
TOTAL FAT: 6.0 g
SATURATED FAT: 1.7 g
TRANS FAT: 0.0 g

CHOLESTEROL: 65 mg
SODIUM: 375 mg
POTASSIUM: 920 mg
TOTAL CARBOHYDRATE: 12 g

DIETARY FIBER: 2 g
SUGARS: 4 g
PROTEIN: 25 g
PHOSPHORUS: 475 mg

BARBECUE SAUCE

SERVES: 18 • **SERVING SIZE:** 1/4 cup • **PREP TIME:** 5 minutes • **COOK TIME:** 20 minutes

1 small onion, minced

2 8-ounce cans tomato sauce

2 cups water

1/4 cup red wine vinegar

1/4 cup Worcestershire sauce

2 teaspoons paprika

2 teaspoons chili powder

Fresh ground pepper

1/2 teaspoon cinnamon

1/8 teaspoon ground cloves

1 Combine all ingredients in saucepan. Add 1 teaspoon salt, if desired. Bring to a full boil. Reduce heat and simmer for 20 minutes.

CHOICES: Free Food
CALORIES: 15

CALORIES FROM FAT: 0
TOTAL FAT: 0.0 g
SATURATED FAT: 0.0 g
TRANS FAT: 0.0 g

CHOLESTEROL: 0 mg
SODIUM: 160 mg
POTASSIUM: 125 mg
TOTAL CARBOHYDRATE: 3 g

DIETARY FIBER: 1 g
SUGARS: 2 g
PROTEIN: 0 g
PHOSPHORUS: 15 mg

CILANTRO SALSA

SERVES: 4 • **SERVING SIZE:** 1/2 cup • **PREP TIME:** 5 minutes + overnight refrigeration

2 tomatoes, diced

1 small cucumber, peeled and chopped

1 small red onion, diced

1/2 cup chopped fresh cilantro leaves

Zest of 1 lime

1 small green pepper, diced

1–2 dashes hot sauce

1 Blend all ingredients to desired chunkiness. Add salt and pepper, if desired, and chill overnight.

CHOICES: 2 Nonstarchy Vegetable
CALORIES: 40

CALORIES FROM FAT: 0
TOTAL FAT: 0.0 g
SATURATED FAT: 0.1 g
TRANS FAT: 0.0 g

CHOLESTEROL: 0 mg
SODIUM: 10 mg
POTASSIUM: 400 mg
TOTAL CARBOHYDRATE: 9 g

DIETARY FIBER: 2 g
SUGARS: 5 g
PROTEIN: 2 g
PHOSPHORUS: 45 mg

HABAÑERO PASTE

SERVES: 48 • **SERVING SIZE:** 1/2 teaspoon • **PREP TIME:** 15–20 minutes • **COOK TIME:** none

1/2 cup water
3 habañero peppers
1 clove garlic, peeled
1/3 cup olive oil

1 Bring water to a boil, then remove from heat. Use a teaspoon to carefully remove seeds and white vein from peppers. If your hands are sensitive to peppers, wear gloves.

2 Soak peppers in hot water for at least 5 minutes. This will help reduce the pepper heat. Drain.

3 In a blender or food processor, blend all ingredients until a soft paste forms. Use small amounts or to taste as directed in different recipes, or add to fresh salsa.

CHOICES: Free Food
CALORIES: 15
CALORIES FROM FAT: 15
TOTAL FAT: 1.5 g
SATURATED FAT: 0.2 g
TRANS FAT: 0.0 g
CHOLESTEROL: 0 mg
SODIUM: 0 mg
POTASSIUM: 0 mg
TOTAL CARBOHYDRATE: 0 g
DIETARY FIBER: 0 g
SUGARS: 0 g
PROTEIN: 0 g
PHOSPHORUS: 0 mg

PESTO SAUCE

SERVES: 16 • **SERVING SIZE:** 1 tablespoon • **PREP TIME:** 10 minutes • **COOK TIME:** none

2 cloves garlic, peeled
1 teaspoon salt
3 cups packed basil leaves, cleaned
2 tablespoons chopped parsley
1/4 cup pine nuts
1/2 cup olive oil
2 tablespoons hot water
1/3 cup freshly grated Parmesan cheese

1 Put all ingredients except cheese in a blender. Blend until smooth, using the hot water to thin out the mixture, and then add cheese. Use on pasta, couscous, rice, or tofu.

CHOICES: 2 Fat
CALORIES: 85
CALORIES FROM FAT: 80
TOTAL FAT: 9.0 g
SATURATED FAT: 1.5 g
TRANS FAT: 0.0 g
CHOLESTEROL: 0 mg
SODIUM: 160 mg
POTASSIUM: 55 mg
TOTAL CARBOHYDRATE: 1 g
DIETARY FIBER: 1 g
SUGARS: 0 g
PROTEIN: 1 g
PHOSPHORUS: 15 mg

SWEET RED PEPPER DIP

SERVES: 16 • **SERVING SIZE:** 2 tablespoons • **PREP TIME:** 10 minutes • **COOK TIME:** 10 minutes

12 small (about 4 ounces each)
   red peppers, cut up and seeds
   discarded
3 tablespoons crushed garlic
2 teaspoons lemon juice

1 Put ingredients in food
   processor, a small amount
   at a time, and process until
   all is blended. Add salt and
   pepper, if desired.

2 In a nonstick skillet over
   medium-high heat, cook
   the mixture uncovered
   until excess liquid is gone,
   stirring every few minutes.

CHOICES: 1 Nonstarchy Vegetable	**CALORIES FROM FAT:** 5	**CHOLESTEROL:** 0 mg	**DIETARY FIBER:** 1 g
	TOTAL FAT: 0.0 g	**SODIUM:** 0 mg	**SUGARS:** 2 g
	SATURATED FAT: 0.0 g	**POTASSIUM:** 150 mg	**PROTEIN:** 1 g
CALORIES: 25	**TRANS FAT:** 0.0 g	**TOTAL CARBOHYDRATE:** 5 g	**PHOSPHORUS:** 20 mg

BLACK BEAN DIP

SERVES: 6 • **SERVING SIZE:** 1/3 cup • **PREP TIME:** 10 minutes • **COOK TIME:** none

15-ounce can black beans,
   drained
1 small onion, chopped
1 small green pepper, chopped
1 clove garlic, chopped
1 1/2 tablespoons red wine
   vinegar
1 1/2 tablespoons olive oil
1/2 teaspoon sugar

1 Combine all ingredients in
   a food processor. Add salt,
   pepper, and hot sauce, if
   desired. Pulse until beans
   are coarsely mashed.
   Season to taste.

	CALORIES FROM FAT: 30	**CHOLESTEROL:** 0 mg	**DIETARY FIBER:** 4 g
CHOICES: 1 Starch, 1/2 Fat	**TOTAL FAT:** 3.5 g	**SODIUM:** 55 mg	**SUGARS:** 2 g
	SATURATED FAT: 0.5 g	**POTASSIUM:** 200 mg	**PROTEIN:** 4 g
CALORIES: 95	**TRANS FAT:** 0.0 g	**TOTAL CARBOHYDRATE:** 12 g	**PHOSPHORUS:** 65 mg

BEAN DIP

SERVES: 6 • **SERVING SIZE:** 1/3 cup • **PREP TIME:** 5 minutes • **COOK TIME:** none

1/4 cup chopped green onion
15-ounce can pinto or kidney
beans
1/4 cup salsa
1/4 teaspoon cumin
Cayenne pepper to taste

1 Combine ingredients in
food processor. Blend until
smooth. Serve with toasted
pita pieces or vegetables.

CHOICES: 1 Starch	**CALORIES FROM FAT:** 5	**CHOLESTEROL:** 0 mg	**DIETARY FIBER:** 4 g
	TOTAL FAT: 0.5 g	**SODIUM:** 275 mg	**SUGARS:** 1 g
CALORIES: 65	**SATURATED FAT:** 0.1 g	**POTASSIUM:** 220 mg	**PROTEIN:** 4 g
	TRANS FAT: 0.0 g	**TOTAL CARBOHYDRATE:** 12 g	**PHOSPHORUS:** 70 mg

EGGPLANT CAVIAR

SERVES: 9 • **SERVING SIZE:** 1/3 cup • **PREP TIME:** 10 minutes • **COOK TIME:** 45 minutes + 3 hours chill time

1 medium eggplant
2 tablespoons finely chopped
onion
1 medium tomato, finely
chopped
1/4 cup sunflower seeds
1 tablespoon lemon juice
2 tablespoons minced fresh
parsley or 1 tablespoon dried
parsley flakes
2 teaspoons wine vinegar
1 tablespoon chopped garlic

1 Preheat oven to 375°F.
2 Prick eggplant with a fork
a few times. Place on oven
rack, with cookie sheet or
foil underneath, and bake
45 minutes. Cool, peel, and
chop finely.

3 Combine cooked eggplant
in a bowl with the
remaining ingredients. Add
salt and pepper, if desired.
Blend in a blender or food
processor until just slightly
chunky. Chill a few hours
to blend flavors.

CHOICES: 1 Nonstarchy Vegetable, 1/2 Fat	**CALORIES FROM FAT:** 20	**CHOLESTEROL:** 0 mg	**DIETARY FIBER:** 2 g
	TOTAL FAT: 2.0 g	**SODIUM:** 0 mg	**SUGARS:** 2 g
	SATURATED FAT: 0.2 g	**POTASSIUM:** 130 mg	**PROTEIN:** 1 g
CALORIES: 40	**TRANS FAT:** 0.0 g	**TOTAL CARBOHYDRATE:** 5 g	**PHOSPHORUS:** 55 mg

HOMEMADE GRAVY

SERVES: 8 • **SERVING SIZE:** 2 ounces • **PREP TIME:** 3 minutes • **COOK TIME:** 2 minutes

3 tablespoons cornstarch
1/2 cup water
1 1/2 cups broth (dilute drippings from a roast or turkey by using mostly water; use salt-free beef or chicken bouillon granules or cubes; or a combination)

1 Dissolve cornstarch in water. Heat broth and add cornstarch mixture. Boil gently for 2 minutes, stirring constantly.

	CALORIES FROM FAT: 0	**CHOLESTEROL:** 0 mg	**DIETARY FIBER:** 0 g
	TOTAL FAT: 0.0 g	**SODIUM:** 1 mg	**SUGARS:** 0 g
CHOICES: Free Food	**SATURATED FAT:** 0.0 g	**POTASSIUM:** 95 mg	**PROTEIN:** 0 g
CALORIES: 13	**TRANS FAT:** 0.0 g	**TOTAL CARBOHYDRATE:** 3 g	**PHOSPHORUS:** 0 mg

CORN RELISH

SERVES: 6 • **SERVING SIZE:** 1/2 cup • **PREP TIME:** 5 minutes + 2 hours chill time • **COOK TIME:** none

2 cups whole-kernel corn
1/2 green pepper, chopped
1/2 red pepper, chopped
1/2 cup red onion, chopped
1 1/2 tablespoons olive oil
1/4 cup vinegar
3–4 packets artificial sweetener
Dash cumin

1 Mix together all ingredients. Chill 2 hours.

	CALORIES FROM FAT: 30	**CHOLESTEROL:** 0 mg	**DIETARY FIBER:** 2 g
	TOTAL FAT: 3.0 g	**SODIUM:** 4 mg	**SUGARS:** 3 g
CHOICES: 1 Starch, 1/2 Fat	**SATURATED FAT:** 1.0 g	**POTASSIUM:** 200 mg	**PROTEIN:** 2 g
CALORIES: 86	**TRANS FAT:** 0.0 g	**TOTAL CARBOHYDRATE:** 14 g	**PHOSPHORUS:** 55 mg

DRESSINGS, SALSAS, & SAUCES

VEGETABLE BROTH

SERVES: 4 • **SERVING SIZE:** 1 cup • **PREP TIME:** 15 minutes • **COOK TIME:** 35–40 minutes

3–4 onions, chopped
4 carrots, sliced
1 tablespoon crushed garlic
2 leeks, sliced
4 celery stalks, chopped
2 bay leaves
6 sprigs fresh parsley
1 sprig fresh or 1 tablespoon
   dried thyme

2 coriander seeds, crushed
1 whole clove
1 sprig fresh or 1 teaspoon
   dried tarragon
1/4 teaspoon cayenne pepper
2 quarts water
Pinch saffron threads

1 Combine all ingredients in a large pot. Add salt and pepper, if desired. Boil. Keep at a gentle boil, with cover slightly ajar, for 35–40 minutes. Broth will reduce to approximately 4 cups. Strain broth and discard vegetables. Freeze in 1-cup portions to use later.

CHOICES: Free Food
CALORIES: 9

CALORIES FROM FAT: 0
TOTAL FAT: 0.0 g
SATURATED FAT: 0.0 g
TRANS FAT: 0.0 g

CHOLESTEROL: 0 mg
SODIUM: 8 mg
POTASSIUM: 45 mg
TOTAL CARBOHYDRATE: 2 g

DIETARY FIBER: 1 g
SUGARS: 1 g
PROTEIN: 0 g
PHOSPHORUS: 5 mg

PEANUT BUTTER CHOCOLATE SHAKE

SERVES: 1 • **SERVING SIZE:** 1 shake • **PREP TIME:** 5 minutes • **COOK TIME:** none

1 cup fat-free milk

1 extra-small frozen banana (less than 6 inches)

1 tablespoon peanut butter

2 tablespoons no-sugar-added powdered chocolate beverage mix

1 Place shake ingredients into a blender and blend until smooth.

CHOICES: 1 Fruit, 1 Milk, fat-free, 1/2 Carbohydrate, 1 Protein, high fat
CALORIES: 285
CALORIES FROM FAT: 90
TOTAL FAT: 10.0 g
SATURATED FAT: 2.3 g
TRANS FAT: 0.0 g
CHOLESTEROL: 5 mg
SODIUM: 255 mg
POTASSIUM: 810 mg
TOTAL CARBOHYDRATE: 41 g
DIETARY FIBER: 4 g
SUGARS: 27 g
PROTEIN: 14 g
PHOSPHORUS: 330 mg

BANANA-ORANGE CHAMPOLA

SERVES: 8 • **SERVING SIZE:** 3/4 cup • **PREP TIME:** 5 minutes • **COOK TIME:** none

1 1/2 cups sliced ripe banana

1 1/2 cups orange juice, no sugar added

4 cups fat-free milk

1/4 teaspoon vanilla extract

1 Blend half of all ingredients until smooth and creamy, then blend second batch. Combine and serve immediately.

CHOICES: 1/2 Fruit, 1/2 Milk, fat-free
CALORIES: 90
CALORIES FROM FAT: 0
TOTAL FAT: 0.0 g
SATURATED FAT: 0.0 g
TRANS FAT: 0.0 g
CHOLESTEROL: 2 mg
SODIUM: 64 mg
POTASSIUM: 380
TOTAL CARBOHYDRATE: 17 g
DIETARY FIBER: 1 g
SUGARS: 15 g
PROTEIN: 5 g
PHOSPHORUS: 140 mg

PINEAPPLE COOLER

SERVES: 9 • **SERVING SIZE:** 3/4 cup • **PREP TIME:** 3 minutes • **COOK TIME:** none

4 cups pineapple juice, no sugar
added

1/2 cup pineapple, fresh or
canned in own juice (drained)

3 cups lemon-flavored soda
water

1 Blend all ingredients
until smooth.

	CALORIES FROM FAT: 0	**CHOLESTEROL:** 0 mg	**DIETARY FIBER:** 0 g
	TOTAL FAT: 0.0 g	**SODIUM:** 20 mg	**SUGARS:** 12 g
CHOICES: 1 Fruit	**SATURATED FAT:** 0.0 g	**POTASSIUM:** 160 mg	**PROTEIN:** 0 g
CALORIES: 65	**TRANS FAT:** 0.0 g	**TOTAL CARBOHYDRATE:** 15 g	**PHOSPHORUS:** 10 mg

CAFÉ MOCHA

SERVES: 1 • **SERVING SIZE:** 1 glass • **PREP TIME:** 5 minutes • **COOK TIME:** none

1/2 cup strong coffee

1/2 cup scalded fat-free milk,
whipped

1/2 teaspoon cocoa

Artificial sweetener to taste

1 Mix coffee and milk in tall
mug and sprinkle with
cocoa and sweetener.

2 To make iced version:
Make drink as described,
but pour into a large glass
with room at the top. Using
a spoon, slowly slide in ice
cubes until drink reaches
the top of the glass.

	CALORIES FROM FAT: 3	**CHOLESTEROL:** 2 mg	**DIETARY FIBER:** 0 g
	TOTAL FAT: 0.0 g	**SODIUM:** 66 mg	**SUGARS:** 5 g
CHOICES: 1/2 Milk, fat-free	**SATURATED FAT:** 0.0 g	**POTASSIUM:** 260 mg	**PROTEIN:** 4 g
CALORIES: 48	**TRANS FAT:** 0.0 g	**TOTAL CARBOHYDRATE:** 7 g	**PHOSPHORUS:** 135 mg

FRUIT PUNCH

SERVES: 12 • **SERVING SIZE:** 1/2 cup • **PREP TIME:** 5 minutes • **COOK TIME:** none

2 cups unsweetened pineapple
   juice, chilled
2 cups cranberry juice
   (100% juice), chilled
3/4 cup orange juice, chilled
3/4 cup club soda, chilled
Ice cubes
Lime and orange slices

1 Combine all ingredients
   in a large punch bowl just
   before serving.

	CALORIES FROM FAT: 0	**CHOLESTEROL:** 0 mg	**DIETARY FIBER:** 0 g
	TOTAL FAT: 0.0 g	**SODIUM:** 10 mg	**SUGARS:** 11 g
CHOICES: 1 Fruit	**SATURATED FAT:** 0.0 g	**POTASSIUM:** 95 mg	**PROTEIN:** 0 g
CALORIES: 50	**TRANS FAT:** 0.0 g	**TOTAL CARBOHYDRATE:** 13 g	**PHOSPHORUS:** 10 mg

SPARKLING CRANBERRY APPLE PUNCH

SERVES: 14 • **SERVING SIZE:** 1/2 cup • **PREP TIME:** 5 minutes • **COOK TIME:** none

2 1/2 cups cranberry juice
   (100% juice), chilled
2 1/2 cups apple juice, chilled
2 cups club soda
2 teaspoons ground coriander
Orange slices
Fresh whole cranberries

1 Just before serving,
   combine juices, soda,
   and coriander in a punch
   bowl. Float orange slices
   and cranberries on top
   for garnish.

	CALORIES FROM FAT: 0	**CHOLESTEROL:** 0 mg	**DIETARY FIBER:** 0 g
	TOTAL FAT: 0.0 g	**SODIUM:** 15 mg	**SUGARS:** 11 g
CHOICES: 1 Fruit	**SATURATED FAT:** 0.0 g	**POTASSIUM:** 55 mg	**PROTEIN:** 0 g
CALORIES: 45	**TRANS FAT:** 0.0 g	**TOTAL CARBOHYDRATE:** 11 g	**PHOSPHORUS:** 10 mg

YOGURT FRUIT SHAKE

SERVES: 3 • **SERVING SIZE:** 3/4 cup • **PREP TIME:** 5 minutes • **COOK TIME:** none

1 medium ripe fruit (peach, banana, or nectarine), peeled, or 3/4 cup sliced strawberries, papaya, or mango or 3/4 cup whole raspberries or blueberries

1 cup plain fat-free yogurt or no-sugar-added fat-free fruit-flavored yogurt

1 cup fat-free milk
1/4 teaspoon vanilla extract
4 ice cubes, crushed
1/2 teaspoon lime juice (if you use mango)

1 Blend all ingredients until smooth and creamy.

CHOICES: 1/2 Fruit, 1/2 Milk, fat-free	**CALORIES FROM FAT:** 0	**CHOLESTEROL:** 5 mg	**DIETARY FIBER:** 1 g
	TOTAL FAT: 0.0 g	**SODIUM:** 80 mg	**SUGARS:** 13 g
	SATURATED FAT: 0.0 g	**POTASSIUM:** 390 mg	**PROTEIN:** 7 g
CALORIES: 80	**TRANS FAT:** 0.0 g	**TOTAL CARBOHYDRATE:** 14 g	**PHOSPHORUS:** 210 mg

FRESH LEMONADE

SERVES: 4 • **SERVING SIZE:** 1 cup • **PREP TIME:** 5 minutes • **COOK TIME:** none

2/3 cup freshly squeezed lemon juice
3 1/3 cups water
8 packets Equal (or other sweetener equal to 1/2 cup sugar)

1 Mix all ingredients. Chill and serve with ice.

	CALORIES FROM FAT: 0	**CHOLESTEROL:** 0 mg	**DIETARY FIBER:** 0 g
	TOTAL FAT: 0.0 g	**SODIUM:** 15 mg	**SUGARS:** 3 g
CHOICES: Free Food	**SATURATED FAT:** 0.0 g	**POTASSIUM:** 90 mg	**PROTEIN:** 0 g
CALORIES: 15	**TRANS FAT:** 0.0 g	**TOTAL CARBOHYDRATE:** 4 g	**PHOSPHORUS:** 0 mg

RECIPE PHOTO ON PREVIOUS PAGE:

Sally Lunn Peach Cake, pg. 190

SWEET POTATO–RAISIN COOKIES

SERVES: 12 • **SERVING SIZE:** 2 cookies • **PREP TIME:** 15 minutes • **COOK TIME:** 12 minutes

1 cup raisins
1/4 cup tub margarine (60–70% vegetable oil, no trans fat)
1 cup sweet potatoes, cooked and mashed
1 egg

1 teaspoon vanilla
2 cups whole-wheat flour
1/4 teaspoon allspice
1/2 teaspoon salt
1/2 teaspoon nutmeg
1/2 teaspoon baking soda

1 teaspoon baking powder
1 teaspoon cinnamon
1/4 cup walnuts, chopped
1/2 cup bran flakes cereal
Nonstick cooking spray

1 Preheat oven to 350°F. Soak raisins in hot water to cover for 5 minutes, then drain.

2 With a mixer, cream margarine, then add sweet potatoes, egg, and vanilla; beat until creamy.

3 In a separate bowl, mix flour, allspice, salt, nutmeg, baking soda, baking powder, and cinnamon. Add gradually to creamed mixture and mix well. Add raisins, walnuts, and bran flakes.

3 Drop onto cookie sheet that has been sprayed with cooking spray. Bake for 12 minutes or until done.

CHOICES: 1 1/2 Starch, 1/2 Fruit, 1 Fat
CALORIES: 180
CALORIES FROM FAT: 45
TOTAL FAT: 5.0 g
SATURATED FAT: 1.0 g
TRANS FAT: 0.0 g
CHOLESTEROL: 20 mg
SODIUM: 235 mg
POTASSIUM: 260 mg
TOTAL CARBOHYDRATE: 31
DIETARY FIBER: 4 g
SUGARS: 9 g
PROTEIN: 5 g
PHOSPHORUS: 155 mg

GRAHAM PUDDING SANDWICHES

SERVES: 32 • **SERVING SIZE:** 1 sandwich • **PREP TIME:** 10 minutes + freeze time • **COOK TIME:** none

1/2 cup natural peanut butter
1 package chocolate sugar-free instant pudding, prepared
64 graham cracker squares
Cinnamon

1 Mix 1/2 cup peanut butter into prepared pudding.

2 Spread 1 tablespoon mixture onto one graham cracker square and sprinkle with cinnamon.

3 Top with another graham cracker square. Place sandwiches on a foil-lined cookie sheet.

4 Freeze. Eat frozen or slightly thawed.

CHOICES: 1 Starch, 1/2 Fat
CALORIES: 94
CALORIES FROM FAT: 31
TOTAL FAT: 3.0 g
SATURATED FAT: 1.0 g
TRANS FAT: 0.0 g
CHOLESTEROL: 0 mg
SODIUM: 122 mg
POTASSIUM: 70 mg
TOTAL CARBOHYDRATE: 13 g
DIETARY FIBER: 1 g
SUGARS: 4 g
PROTEIN: 3 g
PHOSPHORUS: 55 mg

DESSERTS

BAKED RICE PUDDING

SERVES: 4 • **SERVING SIZE:** 2/3 cup • **PREP TIME:** 15 minutes • **COOK TIME:** 50–60 minutes

1 cup fat-free milk
2 eggs, slightly beaten
1 tablespoon sugar
1/8 teaspoon salt
1 teaspoon vanilla
2 cups cooked brown rice (or other whole grain)
1/8 teaspoon fresh grated nutmeg

1 Preheat oven to 325°F.
2 Heat milk in the top of a double boiler over simmering water until surface begins to wrinkle.
3 In a medium bowl, blend together eggs, sugar, salt, and vanilla. Add hot milk gradually, stirring to mix well.
4 Add rice. Pour into four 6-ounce individual custard cups. Sprinkle surface lightly with nutmeg.
5 Set cups in a deep pan; pour hot water around cups to come to within 1/2 inch of tops of cups.
6 Bake 50–60 minutes or until toothpick comes out clean.
7 Remove from heat and from pan. Chill for several hours before serving.
8 Sprinkle with artificial sweetener, if desired.

CHOICES: 2 Starch, 1/2 Fat
CALORIES: 190
CALORIES FROM FAT: 30
TOTAL FAT: 3.5 g
SATURATED FAT: 1.1 g
TRANS FAT: 0.0 g
CHOLESTEROL: 95 mg
SODIUM: 135 mg
POTASSIUM: 220 mg
TOTAL CARBOHYDRATE: 31 g
DIETARY FIBER: 2 g
SUGARS: 7 g
PROTEIN: 8 g
PHOSPHORUS: 210 mg

WINTER FRUIT

SERVES: 16 • **SERVING SIZE:** 1/2 cup • **PREP TIME:** 10 minutes • **COOK TIME:** 15 minutes

15-ounce can juice-packed peach halves, juice reserved
15-ounce can juice-packed pear halves, juice reserved
15-ounce can juice-packed pineapple chunks, juice reserved
15-ounce can juice-packed cherries, juice reserved
1 tablespoon cornstarch
1 tablespoon brown sugar
1 teaspoon curry powder (or cinnamon)

1 Drain fruit and pour reserved juice into a saucepan. Set fruit aside.
2 Combine cornstarch, sugar, and curry powder. Add to juice, stirring to remove lumps.
3 Cook over medium heat until liquid comes to a soft boil, about 2–3 minutes. Lower heat, stirring continuously.
4 Stir fruit into hot mixture and cook until thoroughly heated. Cool and serve.
5 This recipe can be prepared ahead of time and reheated.

CHOICES: 1 Fruit
CALORIES: 64
CALORIES FROM FAT: 1
TOTAL FAT: 0 g
SATURATED FAT: 0.0 g
TRANS FAT: 0.0 g
CHOLESTEROL: 0 mg
SODIUM: 4 mg
POTASSIUM: 130 mg
TOTAL CARBOHYDRATE: 16 g
DIETARY FIBER: 2 g
SUGARS: 14 g
PROTEIN: 1 g
PHOSPHORUS: 15 mg

GELATIN FRUIT PARFAIT

SERVES: 1 • **SERVING SIZE:** 1 parfait • **PREP TIME:** 15 minutes • **COOK TIME:** none

1 package (4-serving size) sugar-free gelatin dessert, any flavor
1/2 cup sliced fresh fruit, any
2 tablespoons whipped topping
Dash cinnamon or nutmeg

1 Prepare gelatin according to package directions. Remove 1/2 cup for this dessert. Reserve the rest for another use.

2 Alternate layers of gelatin and fruit in a parfait glass. Garnish with whipped topping. Dust top with cinnamon or nutmeg.

CHOICES: 1/2 Fruit, 1/2 Fat
CALORIES: 61
CALORIES FROM FAT: 14
TOTAL FAT: 2.0 g
SATURATED FAT: 1.0 g
TRANS FAT: 0.0 g
CHOLESTEROL: 0 mg
SODIUM: 58 mg
POTASSIUM: 135 mg
TOTAL CARBOHYDRATE: 10 g
DIETARY FIBER: 1 g
SUGARS: 7 g
PROTEIN: 2 g
PHOSPHORUS: 60 mg

ITALIAN FRUIT SALAD

SERVES: 6 • **SERVING SIZE:** 1/2 cup • **PREP TIME:** 10 minutes + 2 hours chill time • **COOK TIME:** none

1/4 cup freshly squeezed orange juice
1/4 lemon, juiced and rind grated
1 apple, unpeeled, cubed
1 pear, unpeeled, cubed
1/4 pound seedless grapes
1 peach (if in season), peeled and sliced
1 banana, sliced
2 packets artificial sweetener
1 tablespoon orange liqueur (optional)

1 Combine orange juice, lemon juice, and grated lemon rind in a large bowl. Cut the fruit into the mixture, mixing it with the juice to keep it from discoloring.

2 Add sweetener and orange liqueur, if desired. Toss lightly.

3 Cover bowl with plastic wrap and chill at least 2 hours before serving.

CHOICES: 1 1/2 Fruit
CALORIES: 77
CALORIES FROM FAT: 4
TOTAL FAT: 0.0 g
SATURATED FAT: 0.0 g
TRANS FAT: 0.0 g
CHOLESTEROL: 0 mg
SODIUM: 1 mg
POTASSIUM: 240 mg
TOTAL CARBOHYDRATE: 20 g
DIETARY FIBER: 2 g
SUGARS: 15 g
PROTEIN: 1 g
PHOSPHORUS: 20 mg

FRUIT CRISP

SERVES: 6 • **SERVING SIZE:** 3/4 cup • **PREP TIME:** 10 minutes • **COOK TIME:** 30 minutes

Nonstick cooking spray

3 cups sliced apples

14.25-ounce can juice-packed peaches

1/2 cup oatmeal

1/2 cup whole-wheat flour

3/4 teaspoon cinnamon

3/4 teaspoon nutmeg

3/4 teaspoon cornstarch

2 tablespoons tub margarine (30–50% vegetable oil)

1 Lightly coat a 9 × 9-inch baking pan with cooking spray. Put apples and peaches in pan along with the peach juice.

2 In a separate bowl, combine oatmeal, flour, cinnamon, nutmeg, cornstarch, and margarine. Stir half of mixture into fruit.

3 Sprinkle remainder of the dry mixture over top of the fruit and bake at 375°F for 30 minutes.

CHOICES: 1 Starch, 1 Fruit	**CALORIES FROM FAT:** 20 **TOTAL FAT:** 2.5 g **SATURATED FAT:** 0.6 g	**CHOLESTEROL:** 0 mg **SODIUM:** 30 mg **POTASSIUM:** 200 mg	**DIETARY FIBER:** 4 g **SUGARS:** 13 g **PROTEIN:** 3 g
CALORIES: 140	**TRANS FAT:** 0.0 g	**TOTAL CARBOHYDRATE:** 28 g	**PHOSPHORUS:** 80 mg

BAKED APPLE

SERVES: 2 • **SERVING SIZE:** 1 apple • **PREP TIME:** 15 minutes • **COOK TIME:** 30 minutes

2 small cooking apples

2 teaspoon tub margarine (60–70% vegetable oil, no trans fat)

2 teaspoon low-sugar currant or grape jelly

1 Preheat oven to 350°F. Core apples, leaving bottom intact. Place in ovenproof baking dish with 1/2 inch water.

2 Put 1 teaspoon margarine and 1 teaspoon jelly in each apple. Bake for 30 minutes or until tender. Baste with jelly-margarine mixture before serving.

CHOICES: 1 Fruit, 1/2 Fat	**CALORIES FROM FAT:** 25 **TOTAL FAT:** 3.0 g **SATURATED FAT:** 0.6 g	**CHOLESTEROL:** 0 mg **SODIUM:** 30 mg **POTASSIUM:** 130 mg	**DIETARY FIBER:** 2 g **SUGARS:** 12 g **PROTEIN:** 0 g
CALORIES: 85	**TRANS FAT:** 0.0 g	**TOTAL CARBOHYDRATE:** 16 g	**PHOSPHORUS:** 15 mg

FRESH FRUIT COCKTAIL

SERVES: 6 • **SERVING SIZE:** 1/2 cup • **PREP TIME:** 15 minutes • **COOK TIME:** none

2 large oranges, peeled (strip membrane from each segment and cut into 2–3 pieces)

1 cup papaya, peeled, seeded, and cubed

1 cup ripe mango, peeled and cubed

1/4 cup orange, lime, or lemon juice

6 sprigs fresh mint

1 Mix all ingredients and chill. Garnish with mint leaves to serve.

CHOICES: 1 Fruit	**CALORIES FROM FAT:** 0	**CHOLESTEROL:** 0 mg	**DIETARY FIBER:** 2 g
	TOTAL FAT: 0.0 g	**SODIUM:** 1 mg	**SUGARS:** 12 g
	SATURATED FAT: 0.0 g	**POTASSIUM:** 220 mg	**PROTEIN:** 1 g
CALORIES: 61	**TRANS FAT:** 0.0 g	**TOTAL CARBOHYDRATE:** 15 g	**PHOSPHORUS:** 15 mg

BAKED PAPAYA

SERVES: 4 • **SERVING SIZE:** 1 slice • **PREP TIME:** 5 minutes • **COOK TIME:** 15 minutes

1 medium peeled, sliced papaya

1/2 cup orange, apple, or lime juice

Ground cinnamon

1 cup reduced-fat vanilla ice cream

1 Heat oven to 350°F. Place papaya slices on a nonstick baking sheet.

2 Sprinkle with juice and cinnamon and bake for 15 minutes. Top each slice with 1/4 cup ice cream and serve.

CHOICES: 1 Carbohydrate	**CALORIES FROM FAT:** 22	**CHOLESTEROL:** 13 mg	**DIETARY FIBER:** 1 g
	TOTAL FAT: 2.0 g	**SODIUM:** 27 mg	**SUGARS:** 11 g
	SATURATED FAT: 1.0 g	**POTASSIUM:** 260 mg	**PROTEIN:** 2 g
CALORIES: 90	**TRANS FAT:** 0.0 g	**TOTAL CARBOHYDRATE:** 16 g	**PHOSPHORUS:** 45 mg

PINEAPPLE-OATMEAL CAKE

SERVES: 9 • **SERVING SIZE:** 3-inch square • **PREP TIME:** 5 minutes • **COOK TIME:** 30 minutes

1 1/2 cups quick-cooking oats

1/4 cup artificial brown sugar sweetener

3 tablespoons fat-free dry milk

1/4 cup whole-wheat flour

2 teaspoons baking powder

1/4 teaspoon baking soda

2 teaspoons cinnamon

2 cups crushed pineapple, undrained

2 eggs

1 teaspoon vanilla

2 tablespoons corn oil

Nonstick cooking spray

1 Heat oven to 375°F.

2 Combine all ingredients in a large bowl. Mix well.

3 Coat a 9-inch square pan with cooking spray and pour in mixture. Bake for 30 minutes until top is browned and knife inserted comes out clean.

CHOICES: 1 Starch, 1/2 Fruit, 1 Fat	**CALORIES FROM FAT:** 46	**CHOLESTEROL:** 48 mg	**DIETARY FIBER:** 3 g
	TOTAL FAT: 5.0 g	**SODIUM:** 138 mg	**SUGARS:** 8 g
	SATURATED FAT: 1.0 g	**POTASSIUM:** 160 mg	**PROTEIN:** 5 g
CALORIES: 143	**TRANS FAT:** 0.0 g	**TOTAL CARBOHYDRATE:** 20 g	**PHOSPHORUS:** 210 mg

PEANUT BUTTER BALLS

SERVES: 5 • **SERVING SIZE:** 2 balls • **PREP TIME:** 5 minutes • **COOK TIME:** none

1/4 cup natural peanut butter

2 tablespoons fat-free milk

2 tablespoons fat-free dry milk powder

1/4 cup raisins

4 (2 1/2-inch) graham cracker squares, crumbled

1 teaspoon vanilla

1 Combine peanut butter and milk until well blended. Add remaining ingredients and mix well.

2 Divide into 10 balls and place on a foil-lined cookie sheet. Place in freezer until ready to serve.

CHOICES: 1 Carbohydrate, 1 1/2 Fat	**CALORIES FROM FAT:** 65	**CHOLESTEROL:** 0 mg	**DIETARY FIBER:** 1 g
	TOTAL FAT: 7.0 g	**SODIUM:** 45 mg	**SUGARS:** 8 g
	SATURATED FAT: 1.3 g	**POTASSIUM:** 180 mg	**PROTEIN:** 4 g
CALORIES: 140	**TRANS FAT:** 0.0 g	**TOTAL CARBOHYDRATE:** 14 g	**PHOSPHORUS:** 80 mg

NOODLE PUDDING

SERVES: 4 • **SERVING SIZE:** 1/2 cup • **PREP TIME:** 10 minutes • **COOK TIME:** 30–40 minutes

1 egg
1/2 tablespoon sugar
Dash fresh ground nutmeg
1/8 teaspoon cinnamon
1 1/4 cups broad whole-wheat noodles, cooked until only slightly tender

1/2 tablespoon canola oil
1/2 cup apple juice
1/4 cup raisins
Nonstick cooking spray
1 tablespoon chopped pecans

1 Beat eggs and sugar until fluffy. Add remaining ingredients, except spray and pecans.

2 Pour batter into an 8-inch baking pan well coated with cooking spray. Sprinkle with pecans. Bake in 350°F oven for 30–40 minutes or until browned.

CHOICES: 1/2 Starch, 1 Fruit, 1 Fat
CALORIES: 130
CALORIES FROM FAT: 40
TOTAL FAT: 4.5 g
SATURATED FAT: 0.7 g
TRANS FAT: 0.0 g
CHOLESTEROL: 45 mg
SODIUM: 20 mg
POTASSIUM: 140 mg
TOTAL CARBOHYDRATE: 22 g
DIETARY FIBER: 2 g
SUGARS: 10 g
PROTEIN: 4 g
PHOSPHORUS: 70 mg

MOM'S FAMOUS BREAD PUDDING

SERVES: 6 • **SERVING SIZE:** 1/2 cup • **PREP TIME:** 25 minutes • **COOK TIME:** 45 minutes

1 1/2 cups cubed whole-wheat bread
2 cups fat-free or low-fat (1%) milk, warmed
1 cup egg substitute
2 tablespoons Splenda Sugar Blend for Baking
1 teaspoon vanilla
1/4 teaspoon cinnamon
1/4 teaspoon nutmeg
3/4 cup raisins
Nonstick cooking spray

1 Preheat oven to 350°F.
2 In a large bowl, soak bread in warm milk for 15 minutes.
3 In a medium bowl, combine egg substitute, Splenda, vanilla, cinnamon, and nutmeg. Pour over bread. Add raisins. Stir gently until blended.

4 Coat six 1-cup custard cups with cooking spray. Pour mixture equally into cups.
5 Place cups in a pan filled with enough water to surround but not spill into cups. Bake in water bath about 45 minutes. When done, custard should shimmy when pressed gently.

CHOICES: 1 1/2 Carbohydrate, 1 Protein, lean
CALORIES: 140
CALORIES FROM FAT: 0
TOTAL FAT: 0.0 g
SATURATED FAT: 0.1 g
TRANS FAT: 0.0 g
CHOLESTEROL: 0 mg
SODIUM: 150 mg
POTASSIUM: 340 mg
TOTAL CARBOHYDRATE: 26 g
DIETARY FIBER: 1 g
SUGARS: 20 g
PROTEIN: 8 g
PHOSPHORUS: 120 mg

SALLY LUNN PEACH CAKE

SERVES: 12 • **SERVING SIZE:** 1 slice • **PREP TIME:** 5 minutes • **COOK TIME:** 30 minutes

2 cups whole-wheat flour

3 teaspoons baking powder

1/2 teaspoon salt

1 egg, beaten

3/4 cup fat-free or low-fat (1%) milk

1/2 cup canola oil

1/4 cup sugar

Nonstick cooking spray

4 cups peach slices

1 Preheat oven to 375°F.

2 In a medium bowl, sift flour with baking powder and salt. In a large bowl, combine egg, milk, and oil. Add sugar. Stir in dry ingredients. Do not overmix.

3 Place in loaf pan that has been coated with cooking spray. Bake for about 30 minutes or until toothpick inserted in center comes out clean. Top each slice with 1/3 cup peaches.

CHOICES: 1 1/2 Carbohydrate, 2 Fat	**CALORIES FROM FAT:** 90	**CHOLESTEROL:** 15 mg	**DIETARY FIBER:** 3 g
	TOTAL FAT: 10.0 g	**SODIUM:** 200 mg	**SUGARS:** 10 g
	SATURATED FAT: 0.9 g	**POTASSIUM:** 200 mg	**PROTEIN:** 4 g
CALORIES: 190	**TRANS FAT:** 0.0 g	**TOTAL CARBOHYDRATE:** 22 g	**PHOSPHORUS:** 220 mg

MACEDONIA FRUIT CUP

SERVES: 10 • **SERVING SIZE:** 1/2 cup • **PREP TIME:** 5 minutes + 30 minutes chill time • **COOK TIME:** none

3/4 cup orange juice

4 teaspoons lemon juice

15 seedless grapes

12 cherries, pitted

1 medium apple, thinly sliced

1 medium pear, thinly sliced

1 medium banana, peeled and thinly sliced

1 small plum, thinly sliced

1 medium peach, thinly sliced

1/4 cup honeydew melon cubes

3/4 cup strawberries, stemmed and halved

Sugar substitute (optional)

1 Pour orange and lemon juice into a large serving bowl. Add grapes and cherries. Add remaining fruit and sugar substitute, if desired. Toss well. Chill for 1/2 hour before serving.

	CALORIES FROM FAT: 0	**CHOLESTEROL:** 0 mg	**DIETARY FIBER:** 2 g
	TOTAL FAT: 0.0 g	**SODIUM:** 0 mg	**SUGARS:** 11 g
CHOICES: 1 Fruit	**SATURATED FAT:** 0.0 g	**POTASSIUM:** 220	**PROTEIN:** 1 g
CALORIES: 60	**TRANS FAT:** 0.0 g	**TOTAL CARBOHYDRATE:** 16 g	**PHOSPHORUS:** 20

RAISIN-CINNAMON BAKED APPLE

SERVES: 2 • **SERVING SIZE:** 1/2 apple • **PREP TIME:** 15 minutes • **COOK TIME:** 20–30 minutes

1 large baking apple (Rome, Jonathan, or Granny Smith)
1/4 teaspoon cinnamon
1/2 tablespoon raisins
1/2 of a 12-ounce can diet lemon-lime soda

1 Preheat oven to 350°F. Core apple without cutting all the way through to the bottom. Peel one strip of skin around the top of the apple. Place apple in a small casserole dish sprayed with nonstick cooking spray.

2 Sprinkle the cavity with cinnamon and stuff with raisins. Pour soda over apple.

3 Bake uncovered for 20–30 minutes until apple is soft. Cut in half to serve.

	CALORIES FROM FAT: 0	**CHOLESTEROL:** 0 mg	**DIETARY FIBER:** 3 g
	TOTAL FAT: 0.0 g	**SODIUM:** 10 mg	**SUGARS:** 14 g
CHOICES: 1 Fruit	**SATURATED FAT:** 0.0 g	**POTASSIUM:** 150 mg	**PROTEIN:** 0 g
CALORIES: 70	**TRANS FAT:** 0.0 g	**TOTAL CARBOHYDRATE:** 19 g	**PHOSPHORUS:** 25 mg

STRAWBERRY WHIP

SERVES: 4 • **SERVING SIZE:** 3/4 cup • **PREP TIME:** 5 minutes + 10 minutes freeze time • **COOK TIME:** none

0.3-ounce box sugar-free gelatin
1 cup fat-free plain yogurt
1 cup fresh strawberries

1 Several hours or days before, prepare gelatin according to package instructions. Set in refrigerator until hardened.

2 Beat hardened gelatin with a beater until frothy. Add yogurt and beat gently until mixed. Slice strawberries and stir into mixture. Freeze 10 minutes, then serve.

	CALORIES FROM FAT: 0	**CHOLESTEROL:** 0 mg	**DIETARY FIBER:** 1 g
	TOTAL FAT: 0.0 g	**SODIUM:** 100 mg	**SUGARS:** 6 g
CHOICES: 1/2 Carbohydrate	**SATURATED FAT:** 0.1 g	**POTASSIUM:** 190 mg	**PROTEIN:** 5 g
CALORIES: 50	**TRANS FAT:** 0.0 g	**TOTAL CARBOHYDRATE:** 8 g	**PHOSPHORUS:** 130 mg

FRUITED GELATIN WITH CUSTARD

SERVES: 8 • **SERVING SIZE:** 1 cup • **PREP TIME:** 10 minutes • **COOK TIME:** 15 minutes

0.3-ounce package sugar-free strawberry-flavored gelatin

0.3-ounce package sugar-free orange-flavored gelatin

0.3-ounce package sugar-free lime-flavored gelatin

1 1/2 cups fat-free milk

1/16 teaspoon salt

1 1/2 tablespoons sugar

1 egg yolk, beaten

2 tablespoons cornstarch

1 chunk of lime rind

2 cups sliced fresh fruit (use any one or a combination of strawberries, kiwis, bananas, peaches, oranges, or mangoes)

1 Prepare each gelatin flavor individually according to package directions. Refrigerate until set, then cut into 1/2-inch squares and return squares to refrigerator.

2 In a medium saucepan, heat milk, salt, and sugar over medium heat. Pour a small amount of warm milk in a small bowl. Stir in egg yolk and cornstarch until cornstarch is dissolved. Return the milk mixture to the saucepan.

3 Add lime rind and cook over medium heat, stirring constantly, until mixture begins to bubble and thicken. Reduce heat to medium low and continue cooking for an additional 5 minutes. Remove lime rind. Pour into a bowl and let cool.

4 To serve, spoon each gelatin flavor into 8 dessert cups and top with 1 1/2 tablespoons custard and 1 tablespoon fruit. Repeat the layers, using all remaining ingredients.

CHOICES: 1/2 Fruit, 1/2 Carbohydrate	**CALORIES FROM FAT:** 5	**CHOLESTEROL:** 25 mg	**DIETARY FIBER:** 1 g
	TOTAL FAT: 1.0 g	**SODIUM:** 135 mg	**SUGARS:** 8 g
	SATURATED FAT: 0.0 g	**POTASSIUM:** 180 mg	**PROTEIN:** 4 g
CALORIES: 80	**TRANS FAT:** 0.0 g	**TOTAL CARBOHYDRATE:** 12 g	**PHOSPHORUS:** 115 mg

CHOCOLATE-FLAVORED SYRUP

SERVES: 15 • **SERVING SIZE:** 2 tablespoons • **PREP TIME:** 5 minutes • **COOK TIME:** 3 minutes + 10 minutes cool time

1/2 cup dry cocoa, firmly packed

1 1/2 cups cold water

1/4 teaspoon salt

1/2 cup artificial sweetener

2 1/2 teaspoons vanilla

1 Mix cocoa, water, and salt in a heavy saucepan until smooth. Bring to a boil and simmer gently, stirring constantly, for 3 minutes.

2 Remove from heat and let cool 10 minutes.

3 Add artificial sweetener and vanilla and mix well.

4 Store refrigerated in a jar. Stir well in jar before measuring to use.

	CALORIES FROM FAT: 5	**CHOLESTEROL:** 0 mg	**DIETARY FIBER:** 1 g
CHOICES: Free Food	**TOTAL FAT:** 0.5 g	**SODIUM:** 40 mg	**SUGARS:** 1 g
	SATURATED FAT: 0.2 g	**POTASSIUM:** 45 mg	**PROTEIN:** 1 g
CALORIES: 10	**TRANS FAT:** 0.0 g	**TOTAL CARBOHYDRATE:** 3 g	**PHOSPHORUS:** 20 mg

OLD-FASHIONED BANANA PUDDING

SERVES: 6 • **SERVING SIZE:** 1/3 cup • **PREP TIME:** 15 minutes • **COOK TIME:** none

1-ounce package sugar-free
vanilla pudding mix
2 cups fat-free or low-fat (1%)
milk
12 vanilla wafers
2 large bananas, sliced

1 In a medium pan, combine pudding mix and milk. Cook over medium heat, stirring frequently, until it boils, then remove from heat.

2 Place 2 wafers on bottom of each of six custard dishes. Alternate layers of bananas and pudding, starting and finishing with bananas.

3 Chill before serving.

CHOICES: 1 1/2 Carbohydrate	**CALORIES FROM FAT:** 15	**CHOLESTEROL:** 5 mg	**DIETARY FIBER:** 1 g
	TOTAL FAT: 1.5 g	**SODIUM:** 265 mg	**SUGARS:** 13 g
	SATURATED FAT: 0.4 g	**POTASSIUM:** 300 mg	**PROTEIN:** 4 g
CALORIES: 120	**TRANS FAT:** 0.0 g	**TOTAL CARBOHYDRATE:** 24 g	**PHOSPHORUS:** 220 mg

FROSTY GRAPES

SERVES: 4 • **SERVING SIZE:** 17 • **PREP TIME:** 5 minutes + freeze time • **COOK TIME:** none

1 pound seedless grapes
0.3-ounce package lime sugar-
free gelatin powder

1 Divide grapes into small bunches. Rinse and drain. Put gelatin powder in a container with a lid that can be frozen.

2 Add grapes and shake to coat. Shake off excess powder from grape bunches. Put lid on container and freeze. Serve frozen.

	CALORIES FROM FAT: 0	**CHOLESTEROL:** 0 mg	**DIETARY FIBER:** 1 g
	TOTAL FAT: 0.0 g	**SODIUM:** 60 mg	**SUGARS:** 13 g
CHOICES: 1 Fruit	**SATURATED FAT:** 0.0 g	**POTASSIUM:** 160 mg	**PROTEIN:** 2 g
CALORIES: 65	**TRANS FAT:** 0.0 g	**TOTAL CARBOHYDRATE:** 15 g	**PHOSPHORUS:** 50 mg

DESSERTS

HOLIDAY CRANBERRY ROLLS

SERVES: 18 • **SERVING SIZE:** 1 roll • **PREP TIME:** 30 minutes + 2 hours chill time • **COOK TIME:** 40 minutes

1 package (or 1 tablespoon) active dry yeast
1/4 cup warm water (110–115°F)
1 cup whole-wheat flour
1 1/2 cups unbleached all-purpose flour
1 tablespoon sugar
1/4 teaspoon salt
1/2 cup tub margarine (30–50% vegetable oil)
1/2 cup fat-free milk
2 eggs
1 1/2 cups fresh or frozen cranberries, thawed
1 orange, peeled and sectioned
2 tablespoons dark or light brown sugar
1/4 cup unsweetened applesauce
Nonstick cooking spray
1/2 cup frozen orange juice concentrate, thawed

1 In a small bowl, dissolve yeast in warm water. In a large bowl, combine flours, sugar, and salt. Cut in margarine with a pastry blender or two knives until the mixture resembles crumbs. Add milk, eggs, and proofed yeast. Mix well. Cover and refrigerate for 2 hours or overnight.

2 Meanwhile, prepare the filling by combining cranberries, orange, brown sugar, and applesauce in a food processor or blender. Process until coarse. Transfer to a saucepan and cook over medium heat for 10 minutes. Remove from heat and cool.

3 After chilling the dough, turn it out onto a floured surface. With a floured rolling pin, roll the dough into an 18 × 12-inch rectangle. Spread the filling over the dough, being careful not to spread too close to the edges. Roll the dough jelly-roll fashion. Cut into 18 rolls with a sharp knife. Place in a 13 × 9-inch baking pan sprayed with nonstick cooking spray. Cover with a towel and let rise in a warm place for about 30 minutes, or until doubled in bulk.

4 Preheat oven to 350°F. Bake rolls for 25–30 minutes or until golden brown.

5 While rolls are still warm, glaze with orange juice concentrate.

CHOICES: 1 Starch, 1/2 Fruit, 1/2 Fat
CALORIES: 125
CALORIES FROM FAT: 25
TOTAL FAT: 3.0 g
SATURATED FAT: 0.7 g
TRANS FAT: 0.0 g
CHOLESTEROL: 25 mg
SODIUM: 85 mg
POTASSIUM: 140 mg
TOTAL CARBOHYDRATE: 21 g
DIETARY FIBER: 2 g
SUGARS: 7 g
PROTEIN: 3 g
PHOSPHORUS: 65 mg

STRAWBERRY SHORTCAKE

SERVES: 8 • **SERVING SIZE:** 7/8 ounce cake + 1/4 cup strawberries + 2 tablespoons whipped topping
PREP TIME: 5 minutes • **COOK TIME:** none

1/2 store-bought angel food cake (7 ounces)
2 cups fresh strawberries, sliced
1 cup light whipped topping

1 Cut cake into eight portions. Place each slice of cake on a dessert dish and add 1/4 cup strawberries. Top with 2 tablespoons whipped topping.

CHOICES: 1 1/2 Carbohydrate	**CALORIES FROM FAT:** 15	**CHOLESTEROL:** 0 mg	**DIETARY FIBER:** 1 g
	TOTAL FAT: 1.5 g	**SODIUM:** 135 mg	**SUGARS:** 13 g
	SATURATED FAT: 1.0 g	**POTASSIUM:** 105 mg	**PROTEIN:** 2 g
CALORIES: 95	**TRANS FAT:** 0.0 g	**TOTAL CARBOHYDRATE:** 21 g	**PHOSPHORUS:** 75 mg

RASPBERRY ORANGE GELATIN SUPREME

SERVES: 6 • **SERVING SIZE:** 3/4 cup • **PREP TIME:** 5 minutes • **COOK TIME:** 10 minutes + 1 hour chill time

1 packet orange sugar-free gelatin
1 packet raspberry sugar-free gelatin
2 cups apple-raspberry juice
2 cups water
11 ounces mandarin orange sections, packed in juice, drained

1 Pour gelatin packets into a 2-quart bowl.
2 In a small pan, mix raspberry juice with water and heat to boiling.
3 Mix boiling juice mixture into gelatin, stirring until gelatin is dissolved thoroughly.
4 Chill until thickened but not completely gelled. Add orange sections, stirring to spread throughout gelatin.
5 Chill until firm.

CHOICES: 1 Fruit	**CALORIES FROM FAT:** 0	**CHOLESTEROL:** 0 mg	**DIETARY FIBER:** 0 g
	TOTAL FAT: 0.0 g	**SODIUM:** 80 mg	**SUGARS:** 10 g
	SATURATED FAT: 0.0 g	**POTASSIUM:** 140 mg	**PROTEIN:** 2 g
CALORIES: 55	**TRANS FAT:** 0.0 g	**TOTAL CARBOHYDRATE:** 12 g	**PHOSPHORUS:** 55 mg

Quick Homemade Raisin Bread, pg. B49

INDEX